MAKING A DIFFERENCE

Social Work with Disabled Children

Laura Middleton

VENTURE PRESS

Published by
Venture Press
16 Kent Street
Birmingham
B5 6RD
Tel: 0121 622 3911

First published 1995

British Library Cataloguing in Publication Data

Laura Middleton
Making a Difference: Social Work with Disabled Children

ISBN 1873878 54 0

Printed and bound in Great Britain by
Biddles Ltd, Guildford and King's Lynn

Layout and production management by
Hucksters Advertising & Publishing Consultants
Riseden, Tidebrook, Wadhurst, East Sussex TN5 6PA

To the Next Generation

Contents

Acknowledgements

This book is written for social workers and informed by their experiences and ideas. I would like to record my thanks to all the practitioners and students who contributed to discussions; came to Network meetings; commented at conferences; filled in questionnaires; telephoned; wrote to me or allowed themselves to be interviewed. Their concern to reflect on and improve the quality of social work has made writing this book a project with purpose, and I hope they enjoy reading it as much as I enjoyed talking to them.

I started out with the intention of including research evaluating services since the Children Act from a user perspective and it was with regret that I had to abandon plans which proved too ambitious to complete with any credibility in what was essentially my spare time. The legislation is too new for retrospective evaluation by children who have grown up, and interviewing children currently in receipt of services is not a simple task. Despite my failure to do the business, I remain grateful to those who offered to help. I hope what I have written at least provides some food for thought.

Some of the ideas in Chapter 2 were first published in an article in *Childright* in January 1995 and I am grateful to the editor for permission to repeat them here.

As someone who experiences occasional urges to communicate, I am extremely lucky that my closest friends, Ruth Eley and Ann Gegg are not only experienced and talented social workers, but just love helping out! I know the thrill of encountering my half-baked manuscripts is hard to beat as a way of spending a sunny weekend, and I am happy to have provided them with so much fun! I am hopelessly indebted to both of them for unfailing support, sharing their ideas with me and being willing to challenge mine. Ruth also challenged the grammar-check on my PC so effectively that it is now completely passive.

Thanks are also due to Saleem Gazdar and Peter MacDonald for sharing their concerns with me about the position of disabled black children, Stella Coleman for reading an early draft of a chapter which has since disappeared into electronic heaven, Margaret Flynn for stiffening my resolve when it all seemed too much and Sally Arkley and Mark Pearson for encouraging me in their own inimitable fashions.

Finally, I should like to encourage the next generation of voyagers in continuing a commitment to a universe in which diversity is valued and promoted. I hope this book can boldly contribute to such a future.

Introduction
Life isn't Fair...

This book attempts to develop a theory and practice of working with disabled children which recognises and seeks to address their experience as a human rights issue and attempts to construct a model for social services from a child-centred perspective.

Some children are born with or develop impairments which make them different from the majority of children. They experience discrimination because of that difference and are disabled both by the impairment and by the discrimination. As such, disability is a social construct about which ideas are constantly being developed. 'Disabled' is not a value-free term and provokes negative feelings in many people. One of the achievements of the disability movement is to reclaim the word and enable disabled people to take pride in themselves. Difference should be valued as enriching the fabric of society, not hidden or persecuted as perversity. An optimistic vision of the future would be one in which difference was not disabling at all. We do have a long way to go.

As a society we do not really want to include disabled children. If a child does not fit our definition of normality, and cannot be made to do so, we prefer to keep them out of sight and out of mind. To justify this we label them as 'disabled' and subject them to a segregated upbringing which denies their gender, their sexuality, their race, even their rights as human beings.

> *Treating children as children first is of paramount importance.*
> (Guidance to the Children Act, Volume 6: p2)

In utilising the concept of 'children first' the framers of the Children Act were attempting to place the fact of childhood ahead of the fact of disability as a priority in people's thinking. It recognises that for many disabled children their rights and needs as children are overshadowed by the concentration on their disabling condition, so that their needs as children remain unmet. Worse, the concentration on the disability is widely viewed within the context of a medical model with the disability as the problem for which a solution is sought in terms of therapy or medical intervention. As such the child fast becomes pathologised as disabled and, as such, liable to be excluded from the usual experiences of childhood.

Sooner or later, such oppression is internalised by the child, who is in danger of developing a poor self image resulting from the stigma of being disabled. Such children will learn to blame themselves for the fact that there are some things which they are not able to do.

The attempt to refocus attention on the disabled child as a child first is sometimes misunderstood as meaning that the disability ought to be ignored or is something to be ashamed of. This kind of thinking is equally unhelpful since the disabling condition is very much a part of the child's reality. The key factor is surely that it is the impairment which makes the child different from most other children, and this difference is the vehicle through which they are oppressed. In other words the child is disabled by prejudicial attitudes and by discriminatory actions as much as by any inabilities caused by the impairment itself. Indeed an impairment is not necessarily disabling at all. An understanding of the child's experience as oppression makes the use of the term 'disabled child' more accurate than 'child with a disability' since the latter implies that the child and the disability are somehow separable.

It is worth reminding ourselves that many disabling conditions are less an Act of God than creations of society. Children are born with or develop disabilities due to medical experimentation, poor medical science, inadequate antenatal care, poverty, poor educational standards, the ill health of the mother, smoking or other drug abuse or the physical or sexual abuse of the parent. Neither should we forget that child abuse and neglect cause disability. Since a great deal of disability is a product of the ignorance, carelessness and cruelty of society it might be supposed that there was a moral obligation to compensate its victims. In reality the truth is rather the opposite: once a child is disabled society seems to care less about their fate. Disabled children are expected to ask for charity and pity, and demonstrate their personal need for help, not invoke their right to equality of opportunity.

The Children Act provides 'a legal framework for a new approach' (Guidance to the Children Act, Volume 6: p1). As such it was widely expected to mean improved services for disabled children. Although some Local Authorities have devoted a great deal of energy to organisational change, actual improvements at a service level have been slow to materialise. This failure of legislation may have a range of causes, but the bottom line seems to be that as a society we are still capable of excluding disabled children from the mainstream, both literally and conceptually, and providing a two tier service as if disabled children are not really children at all.

The literal exclusion is obvious. Disabled children are largely invisible to most people because they attend separate nurseries and schools and appear in the media only to attract charitable funding, much like baby seals or victims of natural disasters. In social work terms they are dealt with by separate teams or separate workers, often in medical settings, who have tended to focus less on the commonality of childhood need than on the problems associated with disability. This continuing literal separation is made possible and acceptable by our ability as a society to think of disabled children as falling outside the normal conceptualisations of what it means to be a child.

Separatist thinking means it is also possible to continue to imagine that disabled children have 'special needs'. They do not. A disabled child has exactly the same needs as any other child, and ought to enjoy the same rights. This is not to deny that these needs may sometimes have to be met in different ways since disabled children are different from the majority of children. There is no logical reason why achieving this has to mean segregation. For example, children who achieve mobility by walking and those who do so using mechanical aids can be educated together if arrangements for access and mobility within school buildings are appropriate.

On a policy level this separatist thinking translates itself into childcare documents which omit the particular issues for disabled children from their thinking, either because the authors consider that they are dealt with elsewhere under the guise of 'special needs', or because the authors do not consider disabled children at all.

Worse perhaps is the kind of thinking which so objectifies the child as the problem that their needs are excluded from the picture altogether. An example might help. The following extract is taken from a book considering partnership under the Children Act:

> *Respite care is probably an ideal situation as far as carrying through partnership into the casework relationship is concerned. It exemplifies the type of circumstances where the model of the consumer family using the services of the local authority is most appropriate. There is likely to be a degree of consensus between the social worker and parent about what the problems are and what are the most appropriate measures to deal with them.... The short term break from the stresses of caring for a child with disabilities is by definition what respite care is all about, and it is a good candidate for partnership since there is less scope for the emergence of conflict. It is easier to share power and control in such situations too, where there are not child protection concerns.'*
>
> (Woodhouse 1995: p139)

Clearly, the assumptions in this paragraph can only hold true if the child's wishes are disregarded, the legal requirement to promote the upbringing of children within their own families is subjugated and respite care is regarded as a safe environment.

Respite care is clearly assumed to be a service for parents not children: a premise which will continue into adulthood. The notion that there are no child protection issues involved in the provision of respite care is dangerously naive. Regrettably, from the point of view of disabled children, it is all too common an assumption.

Child protection ought to include all children as having an equal right not to be abused and yet despite their greater vulnerability disabled children have systematically been excluded from consideration at both a policy and a practice level. The Department of Health (1995) publication *Child Protection: messages from research* includes nothing whatsoever about the abuse of disabled children. At a practice level it is common to hear social workers talk of child protection as swallowing up all the resources that could be shared with disabled children, as if the two areas of work were mutually exclusive.

Separatist thinking means that academics and researchers are able to write about issues of childcare, child protection and children's legislation without considering the implications for children who are disabled. The excuse that disabled children are inherently included in any writing about children is not acceptable, any more than a suggestion that black children are automatically included would be. Disabled children are actively discriminated against and any academic, political or research documentation about the needs or rights of children should be expected to address this discrimination.

Where they do include them, the academic community and the social work profession have largely continued to treat disabled children as a medical or social problem and to focus much of their attention on finding ways to help parents seek cure or to cope with it. The child's needs are almost invariably secondary to those of their parents and to those of non disabled children.

There are a number of reasons for wishing to attempt a conceptual shift from seeing disabled children as problems for others towards a child-centred perspective which recognises they are a minority group oppressed because of their impairments.

First, no lasting difference will occur for disabled adults while generations of disabled children grow up learning inferiority, and while society continues to regard them as a pathologised group. Social services is one area where it might reasonably be expected that thinking could change toward valuing disabled children as children in their own right and as citizens of the future. There are issues of inconsistency in current provision across social services and health where children are segregated throughout childhood and then subjected to processes of normalisation to attempt reintegration in adulthood.

Second, the lives of disabled children are being devalued here and now. This not only contributes to a continuing loop of oppression, but has unpleasant day-to-day consequences for those children and for their families.

Third, no fundamental shift in service patterns can occur without an underlying shift in the societal value base. The social model of disability has been of little influence in the design of services for children, which, despite a great deal of reshuffling, remains largely based on a model of individual pathology, for which individual assessment is the usual response. This is neither the most effective nor the most appropriate model. Organisations are resistant to a changed conception of disabled children as subject to discrimination, not simply victims of impairment. At the same time, childcare workers are failing to take sufficient account of basic childcare principles when working with disabled children.

It is logical to suppose that organisations resistant to change or sensitive to criticism will resist new ideas, such as a child-centred approach to disabled children. This book will examine the responses of social services departments to new responsibilities under the Children Act. It will evaluate the effect of the conflicting pressure of legislative demands to integrate disabled children against the informal permission granted by society to continue to marginalise them in service terms. It is arguable that the Children Act looks two ways here, legislating to bring disabled children into mainstream provision at the same time as insisting on a separate definition and requiring the establishment of a Register for disabled children.

The current fragmentation of the social work task into its component parts is also creating divisions which set advocacy against care management, counselling against assessment. All of these are occurring in a theoretical vacuum because of a lack of purpose of social work with disabled children other than a slavish adherence to a medical or pathological model.

This book is an attempt to construct and work within a new framework which recognises and fuses the elements of a social model as it applies to children in the present (not simply as future adults), the impact of childcare principles into the disability field, and the tension between parental, professional and children's interests. It offers a model of social work practice with disabled children and their families which takes due regard of childcare principles and offers a challenge to institutional disabilist practice.

Chapter 1 outlines the legislative demands of the Children Act and offers a commentary on the failure of the Act to meet its own demands. This is followed by two short chapters setting the Act and the position of disabled children into a wider context as recognition that social work does not operate in isolation but within a cultural framework that teaches disabilist attitudes and ways of behaving. Changes to this wider culture will not occur overnight but are probably more likely to happen through the erosion of oppressive attitudes by individuals, communities and organisations of disabled people than from legislative imposition from above. This means that everyone has a contribution to make in the fight to dismantle oppression.

In expressing a need for change, the book suggests that this is most likely to occur in social work within the area of child protection since that area attracts most attention outside the profession. Creating a child protection service that is good enough to include disabled children would mean an improved service for all children since it would mean workers who were better trained in communicating, addressing complex issues and thinking creatively about solutions. There could also be spin offs for services for disabled children beyond child protection since a good child protection service would entail building up preventative services to maintain children at home. There is an urgent need to extend the range of services for disabled children beyond the traditional building based respite which separates families and pathologises the child. Child protection is not a side issue, nor should it be regarded as a specialist concern from which 'disability specialists' can allow themselves to be excluded. Child protection represents a key service at the heart of social work practice with all children, and as such can be an engine for driving change.

The final part of the book approaches social work with disabled children and their families from a child-centred and anti-oppressive perspective. Most writing (and presumably thinking) on anti-discriminatory practice excludes disabled children as an oppressed group, possibly because it would mean addressing the unpalatable possibility that their own parents are part of the oppressive system. The dilemma is to raise the profile of disabled children without ducking the real problems faced by their parents. It means some rethinking about the real source of those problems rather than the current tendency to centre them all on the disabled child. There is a need to develop methods of working with parents that involve partnership and getting alongside, but which do not lose sight of the primary social work responsibility toward the child. This involves changes in practice both at professional level, and at an organisational level, given the necessity to move from a pathological, individual way of working toward an understanding of childhood disability as a vehicle for oppressive professional and organisational practices.

The meaning of oppression

> *Oppression is your belief that you are better than I am, and mine that you might be right.*

Oppression is a strong term, and I hesitated over its use in this book before concluding that it is sometimes necessary to tell it how it is. That it does hit home is evidenced by the vicious mocking reaction of the right wing establishment in its efforts to discredit anti oppressive practice. Nevertheless, some explanation of what I mean by oppression might be useful.

Oppression can range from the merely uncomfortable to intolerance of such magnitude that its victims are killed by it. A newly disabled person who cannot face living any more is one such victim. So is a disabled baby whose doctors or parents decide its life is valueless, and that it should die.

Oppression is not simply the abuse of power by one person or group over others: it is how the oppressed group is made to feel about it, and about themselves. To take a simple example: when I walk alone and have to pass by a man, or a group of youths, I may feel uneasy or afraid. I am aware of their power, and my vulnerability, because I know that men attack women on their own. When I pass by and they do or say nothing, I may feel ashamed of my own fear, and of casting them as possible villains.

Oppression is more than fear of physical violence: it is about some groups in society making the rules and the realities that others are pressured to live by. It concerns a societal belief system about what is normal and acceptable and good, which is internalised not only by those who fit the definitions of normality but also by those who do not. Being oppressed is being made to feel bad about yourself for not fitting in.

In Britain, these societal beliefs are that it is normal to be heterosexual, Christian, white, able-bodied, and to communicate by speaking English. Given these assumptions, it follows that only the deliberately defiant or the very sick will deviate, and society operates very powerful sanctions to discourage such deviance. It is much easier to play by the rules, and not to think too hard about it. Relationships within society are based on the assumption that everyone shares the basic belief system, accepts it and wants to fit in as best they can.

Oppression is being forced to live a life according to someone else's rules, within their reality, and according to their assumptions. The degree and manner to which this is overt and enforced clearly differs from situation to situation. No one pretends that laughing at a child who stutters should attract the same degree of moral revulsion as the mass murder of disabled children in Nazi Germany, but it is nevertheless part of the same continuum of correlating right with might.

Many people contribute to their own oppression and that of others in their group by trying to pass: to pretend to belong to the majority group. They may join in the vilification of their own kind out of either hypocrisy or fear. In some cases certainly, oppressed people believe their own bad press and internalise their own oppression.

At the risk of a broad generalisation, internalising an oppression and fixing it firmly into a negative self-image seem more likely for a person who has grown up with it , and with the negative conditioning of the more powerful section of society, than it is for those who, say, 'discover' their homosexuality as adults, or who become disabled later in life. The risk of internalising an oppression is certainly high for disabled children, not only contributing to their own belief in the superiority of able-bodied people but increasing their vulnerability to abuse through the belief that disabled children are worth less and valued less.

There are members of all oppressed groups who deal with it by trying to pass: some simply out of fear, others because of the knowledge that life is better on the other side of the fence. Disabled people are trying to resist pressure to conform to be accepted. Nasa Begum, who is both black and disabled, writes of reclaiming her identity 'by refusing to accept a concept of "normality" which tells me I must walk, have fair skin and try to blend in by wearing Western clothes' (Begum 1994)

Parents of a disabled child are its best hope for growing up with a positive self-image. Nevertheless, it is also an unpalatable possibility that for disabled children pressure to pass, or normalise, may come from, or at least through, their own parents. The degree of such pressure clearly depends on the parents' own standpoint and attitude, and it is vital to acknowledge that this can change, and that parents can be helped to help their children recognise oppression for what it is, and learn to counter it.

There is clearly grave danger, in raising these difficult issues that parents may become cast as baddies, and the situation is conceptualised in a polarised and fixed way. Such slogans as 'if you are not part of the solution you're part of the problem' are inflammatory and unhelpful. Reality is much more complicated than this. Parents neither constitute the whole of the question, nor the whole of the answer, although many will feel very much left alone to deal with their child. In their relationship with their child they are in turn receivers, reflectors and interpreters of familial, community and societal attitudes. These are all shifting sands.

Finding some fixed and consistent basis for understanding or action can become vital. Some parents do this through existing belief systems. For others the birth and raising of a disabled child will mean change and growth in their own interpretation of life. It is the responsibility of the social worker, in advocating for the child, to encourage a viewpoint which does not pathologise or blame the child, nor assume a fatalistic attitude which assumes that nothing can be done. Religious beliefs can be unhelpful where they explain disability as God-given rather than man-made. The Christian waiting for a miracle is conveniently absolved of the responsibility to seek to change things.

For disabled children there is a complexity of expectation on them, because the pressure comes not simply from society as a whole, but is concentrated and focused often through their own parents. As such, the desire to please is considerably stronger than for an adult disabled person. Where parents can accept their disabled child as she is, and join the disability movement in its fight for her civil and human rights, this particular pressure will ease, but it is sad but true that parents both represent as well as fall victim to, society's disabilist attitudes.

This interpretation of oppression as being deeply rooted within mainstream culture means that anti-oppressive practice has to offer a fundamental challenge to existing values, services, resources and legislation. It may also involve parallel oppressive forces such as racism. As such the task is more than managing individual discrimination, or seeking to ensure that existing rights are acknowledged and respected, although both of these are crucial. Practitioners and organisations must question the basis on which they interact with service users.

Central to underpinning practice with an anti-oppressive approach to disabled children is the conscious adoption of a child centred perspective. This is not normally incompatible with the Children Act principle of partnership with parents since caring parents will also wish to adopt that approach to their children. This concept has attracted its critics, who seem to confuse it with spoiling children, or abdicating responsibility as adults for their well being and upbringing. It is neither. Being child centred means trying to view the situation from the child's perspective, and finding ways forward where possible that are for the benefit of the child: not excusing the cash-strapped school, nor the rest of the street who would prefer the child were hidden from their sight! Seeing the situation from the child's angle means not seeing the child as the problem: to do so is to accept and contribute to her oppression.

This can mean conflict of interest with parents. Situations of overt abuse are, ironically, comparatively easy to deal with since most people accept the wrongness of the action. Much more difficult is where parents genuinely believe, or are made to believe, that they are acting in their child's best interest. It is not at all uncommon for parents to translate the pressure they feel to do their best for their child into a search for the best possible school, or for an elusive, foreign treatment. The terrible dynamics of this mean that the further from home, the more expensive, and the more inconvenient the 'solution' is, the better. In the absence of any real cure, parental commitment to their child is measured instead by the degree of sacrifice, inconvenience and cost they are prepared to bear. Such activity rarely happens in a private way, because it reflects not the child's needs, but those of parents driven to be seen to be 'good'. Local fund-raising is often geared around sending children away somewhere exotic for treatment or education not available in this country. Children are deprived of growing up within a normal family setting, learn that they are not acceptable as they are, and are not allowed to develop along a number of fronts and at a reasonable pace. They have to please their parents by making super-progress in the specified area, which is eliminating the disability, and so justify all the expense and sacrifice. Similar pressures afflict some children sent away to public school.

This is a very vicious circle to break into, since the behaviour is always justified as for the child's own good, even when it breaks up the family, and distresses and stigmatises the individual. Parents need to be released from the pressure, often self-created, to be 'perfect' parents: 'good enough' is all society really should expect.

Parents are also powerful agents of change. They are beginning to demand different and better services for their children. The shortcomings of current provision are less satisfactory when the long-term consequences are better understood: the detrimental long-term effects of special education have to be balanced against the attraction of a safe, quick fix for a young child.

Social work is about change. It involves working with people within their social world and attempting to help them to negotiate it more successfully. This is not to imply that social work is either the only or even the principle agent of change but to acknowledge that its practitioners do hold power in terms of knowledge and skills which can help to make a difference. I hope that this book can assist them in finding ways in which that difference might be a positive one for disabled children.

Part One

The World of Disabled Children

Chapter 1
The Failure of Legislation

The Children Act 1989, henceforth 'the Act', was envisaged as making significant changes to service provision for disabled children by bringing them within mainstream child care, and emphasising that they were 'children first'. The reality has been that change has been patchy and the concept of 'children first' often misunderstood. Instead of being taken to mean that the fact of disability should not override the needs of childhood, it has been used by some to ignore the existence of disability altogether and to assume that policies written with able bodied children in mind will automatically be appropriate for disabled children. This is a mistaken view which takes no account of the discriminatory forces which operate to exclude disabled children from most mainstream activities and services.

The Children Act laid responsibility on local authorities, rather than social services departments, which should mean the development of corporate strategies on disability. This is yet to happen, and it is still all too common to find either neglect of responsibility, or the policies of one department contradicting those of another. An education department which promotes segregated education, for example, is not harmonious with a social services department that has a policy of normalisation. This mismatch can create enormous difficulties as children progress into adulthood. While education and social services are usually seen as the principal players in service provision, local authority departments such as housing, leisure and libraries could be doing a great deal to include provision for disabled children.

The evidence quoted in this chapter is based on research conducted by the author during 1994-5 involving a questionnaire survey of 19 social services departments, and a number of follow-up interviews. All respondents were basic grade social work staff or first line managers. These findings were enhanced and checked out during a series of six network meetings for social workers and team managers working with disabled children held during the same period.

Clearly this is not consumer research, and can tell us nothing about the quality of service as experienced by the children on the receiving end. Such disabled children have yet to be consulted about their views in any meaningful or systematic fashion. As a potential area of research it is fraught with difficulty, not least in effectively separating the views of the child from those of their parents.

Predictably, interviews with parents of disabled children conducted by a research student from the University of Central Lancashire indicate a high level of ignorance about the law, frequently extending to complete unawareness of the existence of the Children Act, and consequently of their rights to services. (Lumb, thesis forthcoming) Such ignorance is largely the result of local authorities failing to provide digestible information, and it increases the responsibility of professional helpers to empower by sharing their own knowledge.

This chapter outlines the basics of what the social worker should know about the Act, relates the principles behind it to service provision for disabled children and then discusses the response of social services to their responsibilities.

Duties under the Children Act

Like all Acts of Parliament relating to local authority services, the Children Act contains both duties and powers. Duties are not negotiable, and may be enforced by legal proceedings such as judicial review. A power simply makes it possible for a local authority to provide a service.

In addition to the Act itself, the Department of Health produced a series of Guidance Handbooks, one of which, Volume 6, deals specifically with disabled children (which it calls 'children with disabilities', presumably to separate the child from the disability). Most of the focus on disabled children is contained within Part III of the Act, which deals with Children in Need; specific duties and powers are listed in Schedule 2 to the Act. Despite this emphasis it is important not to lose sight of the fact that the whole Act applies to disabled children. This is easily forgotten, since the Department of Health segregates disability and produces separate guidance notes. Workers disinterested in disabled children are rarely confronted with the need to include them, as the chances are that Volume 6 is only read by those with some previous commitment or awareness.

Pressure to include disabled children within any mainstream activity, from swimming baths to libraries to child-minding, may come from various sources, but would be most effective from parents. This pressure to make demands is less likely from parents of disabled children for a variety of reasons, perhaps not least of which is their social conditioning not to make a fuss about a problem child. Another powerful demotivator is ignorance of the facilities and lack of awareness of the responsibilities of local authorities. Services for an ignorant service user group are the more easily rationed. Nonetheless, the Children Act contains a clear duty to inform.

Schedule 2, paragraphs 1 (2) (a) and (b) requires local authorities to publish information provided by themselves and others, and to *ensure* it reaches those who might benefit from services (my emphasis). This is a tall order for local authorities, and it is therefore unsurprising to find parents still in ignorance of services provision.

In practice, publishing information is expensive and seen as likely to increase demand, which hard pressed authorities wish to avoid. Worse, it would reveal the paucity of service provision and choice in many areas. Authorities should be pushed to comply with this section of the Act. It may well prove that the accurate provision of information could save time in the long term by enabling people better to focus their demand. It is probable that demand is restricted currently less by lack of need than by the poor image many people have of social services and social workers: an impression that will be reinforced by many of the poor reception facilities which still disgrace many authorities.

Schedule 2 of the Act places a duty on local authorities to maintain a register of disabled children, which some authorities argue is the route to parents receiving information, but this is a circular argument, and reinforces the view that services for disabled children have to be separate from those for children in general.

Difficulties in gaining access to information are compounded for those whose first language is not English. Coming to information later, or not at all, exacerbates problems since action to alleviate difficulties is not taken. This applies along the whole spectrum from medical intervention, practical assistance, education and tackling issues such as racism and disabilism.

It is a requirement of the Act that a local authority must give due consideration to the child's religious persuasion, racial origin, culture and language in making decisions (s.22 (5) (c)). This applies no less to disabled black children as to non-disabled black children. Black people, like any minority group, need support from a 'community' or group where explanation of difference is unnecessary. A disabled black child is in great jeopardy here, since she is likely to be in the hands of non-disabled, white professionals, who are focusing not on race but on disability. Such workers can effectively rob the child of her blackness.

The Act contains a new general duty on local authorities to safeguard and *promote* the welfare of children in need (s.17 (1) (a); (my emphasis). This is a very broad duty, open to interpretation, which has to be understood and put into practice in the context of the Act as a whole. First, it is necessary to understand what is meant by children in need. The Act defines this group as follows:

> *(a) those unlikely to achieve or maintain, or have the opportunity of achieving or maintaining, a reasonable standard of health or development without the provision of services;*
>
> *(b) those whose health or development is likely to be significantly impaired, or further impaired, without the provision of such services;*
>
> *(c) those who are disabled.*
>
> *Development means physical, intellectual, emotional, social or behavioural and 'health' means physical and mental.*
>
> (s. 17(10))

The definition of 'disabled' is lifted from the 1948 National Assistance Act, and one can only assume the framers of the Children Act thought it adequate.

> *...a child is disabled if he is blind, deaf or dumb or suffers from mental disorder of any kind or is substantially and permanently handicapped by illness, injury or congenital deformity or such other disability as may be prescribed.*
>
> (s. 17(11))

The wording of these definitions gives local authorities ample scope for interpretation, and justification for widening or restricting access to services. Using categories of disability to determine access to service rather than looking at the overall picture can mean some children with mild impairments, but whose family are experiencing difficult circumstances, fall out of the frame and are denied any help. The inclusion of the term 'substantial', in particular, has been used to ration access to services by limiting their availability to those with severe disability, in medical terms, whatever the individual needs of the families may be. Families who feel cheated in this way could resort to demanding service under (a) or (b), above, where the argument will revolve instead around the meaning of 'reasonable' or of 'significant'. The truth is that the Act allows local authorities to make substantial services available to a wide range of children, if it so wishes and if it can afford to. Both these conditions have to be fulfilled for any meaningful change to occur. My anxiety is that lack of resources becomes the excuse, where the real reason is lack of will or lack of awareness of what safeguarding and promoting the welfare of disabled children should involve. As will become clearer later, many services are inadequate not because of lack of resources, but because they are poorly matched to need, and do not conform to sound childcare principles. It is worth remembering that poor services also cost money, as do ill-conceived pieces of legislation. The community charge fiasco was a prime example of this. While less spectacular, and less well publicised since it affects a neglected minority, the local authority register of disabled children is equally ill conceived. (Schedule 2, part 2).

The register is the dedicated bureaucrats dream. It combines a clear and simple duty that even the most obtuse can understand with a tangle of ethical and procedural difficulties which allow it to take for ever to establish and keep up to date. An inordinate amount of staff, and perhaps parent time, will be spent arguing around definitions and meanings in order to provide material for it.

Maintaining a register involves categorising certain children as 'disabled', using a definition which is imprecise, but which carries the implication of the child being problematic and legally 'in need'. I have yet to hear a sensible argument which justifies such an infringement of civil liberties. Maintaining records of people who use or ask for services is one thing. Even keeping anonymous statistics of characteristics of the population as a whole is reasonable, if not necessarily renowned for accuracy. Keeping a register of one section of the population because they are perceived, as a whole group, as being problematic for society is quite another. If the requirement had been for a register of smokers, for example, or of black children, the public outcry would have been loud and justifiable. That it is defended for disabled children is at once a measure of their marginality, even lack of perceived humanity, and an indication of the influence of the medical model in conceiving of disability as the primary and pathological characteristic of a child.

Authorities do not need to explain, of course, because keeping a register is a legal requirement. Where they do attempt such explanation, it is usually on the lines of 'for planning purposes'. This is chilling in the extreme, since it suggests they have some preconceived notion of what the future holds in terms of needs of disabled children, and adults, for services. Given the apparent lack of imagination of many authorities this can only mean preprogramming children either for day care or for its current substitute of everlasting further segregated education. Nor does such reasoning explain how local authorities manage to 'plan' for groups for whom they are not required to maintain a register.

It should be borne in mind that while the authority has a duty to maintain a register, there is no equivalent requirement on a parent to register their child, nor is service provision dependent on it. This has resulted in at least one local authority maintaining two sets of data: the official register of willing parents, and the unofficial *list* of those who refuse. This silly situation had arisen out of an ethical concern to give parents some real choice about being registered, and the fault seems to lie less with the authority in question than in the legislative requirement itself.

It would serve the interests of disabled children better if records were maintained of unmet need following thorough and open-minded professional assessments, of which more later! The Children Act does not lay down any procedures for assessment but the Guidance to the Act refers local authorities to the NHS and Community Care Act practice guidance. The need for assessment is implicit in the requirements in Schedule 2 to register and to identify appropriate services. If the authority does decide to assess the needs of a disabled child for service, the parents may request the authority to carry out an assessment of their ability to care under the Carers (Recognition and Services) Act 1995, which the authority must conduct.

Disabled children are entitled to assessment under other legislation: the 1986 Disabled Persons Act, for example, and the 1993 Education Act if the child falls within its definition of special educational needs. In the latter case social services departments have to be consulted by education departments, and should consider a combined assessment.

Schedule 2, Part 6 of the Children Act lays a duty on local authorities to provide services for disabled children to minimise the effects of their disability, and to give them the opportunity to lead lives as normal as possible. This is curiously worded, arising from a medical model that assumes that disability is abnormal and the problem. As such, the duty to minimise the effect of disability can be easily and thoughtlessly translated into a provision of respite to support parents in dealing with *the problem.* In other words, it is interpreted as meaning to minimise the effect of the disability on the parents, not the child. It fails to appreciate the abnormality of most respite as a provision for children, especially young ones. Nor does it show any understanding of the pressures that *maximise* the effects of disability, in following the Act's own logic. Disabled children are prevented from leading normal lives less by their impairments than by barriers in the communities they live in. It is vital for any decent service provider to make the effort to identify barriers in their own area, and within their own services, which prevent disabled children from participation. These rarely stem from the disability itself, but relate to artificial physical constraints, and to discriminatory attitudes on behalf of service providers. This applies much more widely than to social services, or even to local authorities. Barriers exist in a wide range of areas which offer facilities to children and families. Accessing such facilities may involve some strong advocacy toward public bodies if only to remind them of their legal obligations, but given that many of these barriers exist as a result of ignorance or fear of disability, there is also a clear educative role.

It is worth remembering that, at the time of writing, no legislation exists in this country outlawing discrimination on the grounds of disability, unlike that relating to sex and to race. In order to obtain services or facilities disabled children currently have to present arguments for access on the basis of individual *need*, and thus emphasise their own inadequacy, and stress that the spirit of the Children Act is to enable them to lead lives as normal as possible. This failure in the legislative framework means that disabled children have to maintain continual moral pressure to realise what in any just society would be enshrined in law as their rights.

Some hope should lie in the duties to ascertain where reasonably practicable the child's wishes and feelings, and to give these due consideration in making decisions. (s.22(4)(a) and s.22(5)(a)) The weakness here is the 'where reasonably practicable', which provides an excuse for those who maintain a belief that a disabled child cannot communicate, or that it would be too much trouble to try. If this duty were taken seriously, no child would be subjected to institutional respite if they indicated their distaste by bedwetting, refusing to eat, disturbed sleep, refusing to pack or running away from the social worker when they came to take them away. It does not require speech to communicate unhappiness. In practice, the Social Services Inspectorate (SSI) have found it rare for the wishes of disabled children to be either sought or recorded. (Children Act Report HMSO 1993). This is not a matter of resources: it is an issue of bad practice, and a continuing pattern of pathologising the disabled child as the problem, which can be solved by its removal from the home. The principle of paramountcy of the welfare of the child and the duty to provide services to minimise the effects of disability are both lost.

The Act requires the promotion of the upbringing of children by their families (s.17(1)(b)) by providing services such as advice, guidance, counselling, financial assistance or practical help. The Act asks for respect for the cultural background of children. Yet stereotyping of disabled children is all too common and is worse for most children from minority ethnic groups. The stereotypes can contradict each other: Asian families are characterised both as 'looking after their own' and as neglectful of disabled children. These racist assumptions are compounded by lack of black and Asian staff, language barriers, low awareness of services and entitlements, ethnically insensitive or inflexible service provision and racist attitudes among service providers.

Family centres are specifically mentioned as ways of providing occupational, social, cultural and recreational facilities as well as advice for children and parents. There has been little progress in such centres as resources for disabled children, where the duty to *promote* the upbringing of children by their families seems largely ignored. Residential respite care is often justified as maintaining a child in their family, by supporting the parents, but it is a flawed argument. A child in respite is clearly not with their family. Some disabled children are cared for as much by respite carers as by their own family. This flies in the face of the principles of the Act, and distinguishes the care of disabled children from non-disabled children, who are more likely to spend the time with relatives. The opportunities to open up friendship networks are lost for disabled children who spend so much time in segregated care, reached on segregated transport. A disabled black child is particularly vulnerable to being the odd one out if placed in an institutional setting. Residential schooling is another apparently benign way of bringing up children, but this contradicts the imperative to promote their upbringing at home. Some children are placed in euphemistically termed 52-week placements, which are somehow seen as all right because they are conceptualised as in school and not as in care.

It follows that relatives of disabled children want and expect them to move on into residential or institutional respite care programmes when they become adults. Both relatives and children are conditioned into dependency.

I keep returning to institutional respite as an example of bad practice, in the main because in many areas it is still all that is on offer. As such, resourcing it prevents the development and promotion of more imaginative support services, which the non-disabled take for granted, such as after-school clubs, summer play schemes and a range of leisure based activities. There are options which follow more normal patterns of childcare in this country, and may support the parents without the need to remove the child from home.

Some social services departments are beginning to offer a wider range of services. Schemes, which go under various titles from 'link' to 'befriending' are developed to pay for 'friends' for disabled young people to help them access community facilities or visit others, while relieving the parents of care for the day or evening. The scheme with which I am most familiar is run as an adjunct to the fostering and adoption service, and all the paid workers are police checked in the same way as other childcare workers.

Some voluntary organisations are encouraging more normal friendships through schemes which address both psychological and physical barriers which prevent children from meeting and playing together.

Home sitting services provide the opportunity for respite for carers, while not requiring the child to leave home. These need to be flexible. The Crossroads scheme that insisted as a condition of service that the carers went out of the house while the sitter was there denied the parent what she may really have wanted: a long bath, a loud radio and a large gin and tonic. Some parents resist home sitting services, despite an acknowledgement that is more normal for their child (especially for young children), because of sensitivities about their housekeeping standards, or a felt need to clear up before the sitter arrived. These misplaced priorities, which put the parent's need to appear a competent housekeeper ahead of being a caring parent, require some sensitive counselling.

The local authority is obliged by the Act to provide accommodation for any child in need under certain circumstances. These include when the person caring for the child is prevented permanently or temporarily, for whatever reason, from providing suitable accommodation or care. (s.20 (3)) This clearly includes parents who are stressed out or over-tired. The problem is that, if the child is disabled, the next steps in the legal process are often skipped over. Instead of asking the local respite home for a bed, the next step ought to be to ascertain the child's wishes and give due consideration to them (s.22(5)(a)). Accommodation should offer a sense of permanence and security, where the child can experience ordinary family life, have appropriate education, develop a positive self-image and provide opportunities for personal growth (Guidance to the Act, Volume 3). If possible the placement should be with a person connected with the child, such as a parent, relative or friend (s.23 (6)). Failing this, the placement should be near the child's home (s.23(7)(a)), with due consideration given to religion, race and language.

The precedence given to disability rather than the race of the child means a child from a minority racial background is likely to be shipped to the same respite care institution as any other child in the catchment area, the fact of disability taking an easy precedence in allocating the service. Same race placements are now widely accepted as good practice in adoption and fostering. How likely is this consideration to be paramount for a disabled child?

A reasonable test of the quality of service provision is to ascertain whether respite care is offered as an option alongside other services, or on a 'take it or leave it' basis. Where accommodating the child becomes the preferred option, is there a choice of placement so that individual needs and preferences can be met? Older children are more reasonably accommodated away from home than young ones: is there provision for teenagers distinct from that for young children on the one hand, or adults on the other? Or does the authority fall into the common trap of denying that disabled children experience adolescence? Needless to say there are examples of good and bad practice and social workers will be able to rate their own authority accordingly.

Other characteristics of bad service provision apply more widely than to disabled children alone, but they are worth noting. Professionals who are ignorant, unreliable, patronising and judgemental do not help anyone. Services which have long waiting lists, take ages to process requests and make the service user feel inferior, abnormal or inadequate while they are waiting are also ill regarded, as are those which demand that people exaggerate and medicalise their problems in order to receive any attention. While it has to be tempered with some common sense, people dislike having to fit themselves around the needs of the service provider rather than receiving a genuinely flexible service geared to their needs. Finally, compliance and gratitude can become a strain. Getting these things right will not only benefit disabled children, but all service users.

Principles of the Children Act

The general principles which underpin the Act apply equally to disabled children, as do the more detailed childcare principles listed in the Department of Health Guide *The Care of Children*. (DOH 1991b).

The basic general principles of the Act are:

1. The welfare of the child is paramount.

2. Partnership with parents.
3. The importance of families for bringing up children.
4. The importance of the views of parents and of children.
5. Corporate responsibility. The Act relates to the local authority as a whole, not just the social services.

Volume 6 adds that treating children as children first is of paramount importance. This requirement has been widely quoted and widely misunderstood, perhaps deliberately, as a reason to ignore the fact of disability as part of a child's experience. This avoids the necessity to face dealing with discrimination, and makes as much sense as did handling race issues by pretending that colour did not matter.

The Care of Children lists 42 childcare principles which should underpin interpretation and enactment of the legislation by social services departments. It is sad but unsurprising that these principles are more readily applied to some children than others, on the Orwellian premise that some children are more equal than others. Nonetheless, they do perhaps offer one of the best hopes for the future for disabled children, since, if they were applied as rigorously, it would be clear that childcare services consistently fall short when applied to this group. At the risk of immediately unstitching my own argument, I should also state that I am not suggesting the care system always (or even usually) works effectively for non-disabled children.

I do not intend to work through all 42 principles, but the following sample should give an adequate flavour of the mismatch between principles and practice (numbering from original).

> *1. Children and young people and their parents should all be considered as individuals with particular needs and potentialities.*

There is a tendency to categorise disabled children and separate them in terms of service delivery. This leads to routine responses and standardised procedures, which usually exclude consideration of race and culture since disability takes precedence.

> *3. Children are entitled to protection from neglect, abuse and exploitation.*

Disabled children are at greater risk of abuse than non-disabled, from a wider range of people and in a wider range of circumstances. They are more vulnerable and less valued. Yet they are frequently excluded from mainstream child protection textbooks, training or service provision. A woman who chairs child protection case conferences for a large division of a social services department told me recently she had not chaired a single conference in the last twelve months involving a disabled child. This is institutional disablism of the most worrying kind.

> *5. There are unique advantages for children in experiencing normal family life in their own birth family and every effort should be made to preserve the child's home and family links.*

It is much more likely that disabled children will be sent away from home for reasons which relate purely to the disability. Disabled babies and young children are sent for respite. Disabled children are often educated away from home, sometimes on the basis of 52-week placements. These would be seen as permanent care if the child were non-disabled, and planned for accordingly. Despite the principle stating that 'every effort' should be made to preserve links, it is not uncommon for such services to be offered on a 'that or nothing' basis.

> *9. If young people cannot remain at home, placement with relatives or friends should be explored before other forms of placement are considered.*

Support for the extended family is lacking and often not explored where the child is disabled, and there is a standard service response. Residential respite is organisationally easier and more acceptable because the child is 'damaged'.

> *13. Siblings should not be separated when in care or when looked after under voluntary arrangements unless this is part of a well thought out plan based on each child's needs.*

Relationships with disabled children and their siblings are often devalued or stereotyped into 'problem' and 'young carer'. Siblings often go to different schools, and the disabled child is singled out as the one who goes away for respite, or has holidays separately from the family.

One local authority in the survey got around the issue of separating children by offering their respite services to all the children in a family where one was disabled and qualified for respite. This raises some difficult questions, which can only be answered by assessing the needs of all the children in the family, and their relationships with each other. Siblings of disabled children may get on well with them, or not, as with any other sibling relationship. While using institutional respite could be conceptualised as compounding the error of removing children needlessly from the family home, it may be preferable to singling out the disabled child, if no options to such removal can be found. Given the tendency to passivity of disabled children who are conditioned not to make demands, taking non disabled siblings along will almost certainly mean the provider having to be much more conscious of the quality of service, since the non disabled children are likely to be more vociferous if they are not enjoying themselves. Simply being out of the way to give their parents a break is less likely to suffice as explanation for a child who does not have a negative self-image.

> *17. Change of home, caregiver, social worker or school almost always carries some risk to a child's development and welfare.*

Disabled children experience a wide range of care givers. This increases the risk of child abuse. Ironically, special schools, which often cater for children from primary to secondary age groups may provide the most stability on a long-term basis. Sending disabled children away to give their parents a break deprives them of the opportunity to develop ordinary friendships in their own localities.

> *20. All children need to develop self confidence and a sense of self worth, so alongside the development of identity, and equally important is self esteem.*

Disabled children often grow up with spoiled identities because they are treated as problems, separated from their families, forced into mocking able-bodied behaviour, educated separately and denied information. Disabled school leavers typically make low demands, and are unclear what they want from life. A disabled black child is more vulnerable to being isolated from other disabled black children, and may develop no positive sense of black identity at all.

> *21. Since discrimination of all kinds is an everyday reality in many children's lives, every effort must be made to ensure that agency services do not reflect or reinforce it.*

Services typically operate to a medical model, which focuses on the disability before the child, and sees the whole as a problem. Children's identities are medicalised, and they are categorised by their diagnosis. Local authorities now keep registers of such children, and regard them as automatically 'in need'. Agencies as they currently operate do not routinely work within an anti discriminatory framework in their dealings with disabled children.

25. Young people's wishes must be elicited and taken seriously.

As children or adults, disabled people are less likely to be taken seriously than non disabled people.

The overall picture is one where it is clear that different standards are allowed to apply where the child is disabled: the concept of children first, or of a child-centred service, is subjugated to routine service delivery which pathologises the child because of their disability. An acid test is recommended to social workers before they recommend any service to a disabled child: would they consider the same solution if the child were not disabled? If not, why not? To answer such a question with 'because she is disabled' betrays a thinking process which is discriminatory, and fails to see the child as a child first.

The Act treats issues of disability from a traditional perspective, which is still largely adult and able bodied in its conception and framed with enough ambiguity of definition and wording to permit authorities who show little commitment to carry on as before. There is nothing in the Act which addresses the pathologisation of disabled children, and which could be a long enough lever to shift thinking radically. This is not helped by the new Carer (Recognition and Services) Act 1995, which is equally insensitive in its framing.

This Act comes into force in April 1996, and at the time of writing (August 1995) guidance on the Carers Act is still awaited. The Carers Act does not refer to parents as such, nor does it define carer, but Section 1 (2) makes specific reference to individuals who 'provide a substantial amount of care on a regular basis for the disabled child' and states that they can ask for an assessment of their 'ability to provide care'.

In redefining the parents of disabled children as carers, the Carers Act reinforces the message that bringing up disabled children is a harder and conceptually different task from normal parenting. It ought to be possible to provide extra support for parents whose children have high dependency needs without redefining them as carers, which reinforces the children as problems.

The response of social services to the Children Act
The Children Act produced a great flurry of activity in social services departments. It was enacted just before the National Health Service and Community Care Act 1990, which involved departments in radical rethinking of patterns of service delivery, and many social services departments found themselves wrestling with the implementation of these two major pieces of legislation at much the same time, with inevitable conflicts of interests and priorities. Restructuring, the usual recourse of troubled organisations, was endemic. The only major differences involved the timing and speed of change, since some Labour-controlled authorities maintained a faith right up until the last minute that community care would not really happen: that either a Labour government or an eleventh hour move away from local authorities to the Health Service as the lead agency would save them.

There are many who thrive on restructuring: certainly it can provide a sense of purpose to enough managers in most organisations to ensure that the vast majority of the workforce are kept in an unhappy and compliant state of uncertainty for as long as possible. As far as the Children Act was concerned, the opportunity for empire building by Assistant Directors (childcare) at the expense of their colleagues in adult or disability services was irresistible to many. Services for disabled children, however poor, were briefly the focus of attention. At such opportune moments, it was possible for committed managers and practitioners who had enough networking ability within their organisations to make an impact on services. Many of the new services which did emerge in local authorities were born in the general chaos of restructuring, and depended very much on individuals who were around to drive them.

This kind of opportunistic, individually driven pattern of change has meant a very different picture of services in different authorities, but there are some general trends which can be tentatively pulled out. These are derived from questionnaire responses, a research tool which is notoriously unreliable. I can only plead that my questions were very open! I offer these observations not as the definitive conclusion, but in order to try to understand the emergent patterns of change.

Early indications are that change is piecemeal, untidy, cost conscious, management driven and heavily dependent for its character on existing service patterns. Most organisations do not appear to have gone back to the drawing board so much as to have adapted existing services. In some areas, nothing more than a management reshuffle has been thought necessary to achieve the integration of service by transferring line management responsibility. Others have sidestepped the imperative to integrate by setting up specialist teams, an issue that will be discussed in more detail later.

Smaller authorities seem better able than larger ones to get their act together. Communication across larger authorities is more difficult, particularly given the vertical nature of information flows typical in hierarchical structures. In two large social services departments, one urban and one rural, I found staff working to develop services in different areas of the city or county respectively, who were unaware of each others existence until I put them in touch. Given that developing services for disabled children is a minority interest, this is particularly sad, and the chances are high that these two authorities are not untypical.

The means of delivery has usually preempted any debate about what sort of services are appropriate. Little attention appears to have been devoted to developing organisational ideas about what a service could or should look like, nor what it is meant to achieve.

There is no underlying understanding or acknowledgement of such issues as poverty, class or race which should inform planning. Instead, service plans are simply extrapolations based on population categorisations, and crude divisions into severity of disability. Failure to acknowledge the importance of wider forces within society has precluded the funding of any significant research into the needs of disabled children which extends conceptually beyond a medically driven, pathological framework.

It is unusual to find any statements of intent that include any understanding, or even awareness, of the social model of disability. Indeed, childcare workers indicate that they feel disempowered by ignorance of medical conditions: a lack of confidence based on a mistaken view of the purpose of social work.

Respondents to the survey who felt change was management driven were usually being uncomplimentary, and believed managers did not share an understanding with either practitioners or service users. Some quotations are illuminating:

> *'At grassroots level we're unclear about what senior management are planning or aware of.'*

'There is a big gap with what management think and what is going on. Often they are out of touch.'

'I feel management want to attempt to fulfil their statutory responsibilities even if that continues to isolate children with disabilities.... Workers have little say, parents have less and children in some cases have none and are not even asked.'

'Management are budget led, and not needs led.'

'Managers are only too relieved to believe rhetoric and not examine families' experience.'

There is evidence both of woolly thinking, and of incompatible aims and objectives. Nice words are scattered like confetti in policy documents, but they are often high-minded concepts which in practice operate against each other: For example, two popular and incompatible aims are equal opportunities and choice. No system designed to be equitable can permit everyone a free choice.

Policy documents are often so much rhetoric, and it is perhaps unwise to get too concerned about them, but the lack of a coherent overt purpose to many social services is worrying, since it suggests the possibility of the existence of a covert purpose, or conspiracy.

If you start from the actual outcomes of social services, it is possible to suppose that they are designed to hide disabled children, and to build and reinforce the belief that they are of less value, to protect the interests of the non disabled majority. It has even been suggested to me by a social worker that there are institutional interests within adult social services provision that require a steady flow of compliant disabled people to keep them going as viable propositions. While she had her tongue in her cheek, it so closely resembles the pressure to keep special school places topped up that it is difficult to discount altogether.

The idea that poor service may result from deliberate policy, open or covert, is disregarded by many who maintain a view that local authorities are simply not that efficient. Inefficiency as a framework for understanding is based on the notion that social service departments have only the vaguest idea about the effectiveness of their services, and are deluded about the mismatch between stated aims and actual outcomes. If this is the case, the answer lies in educating them to think differently and shake away complacency. Elected members may need convincing that there are votes at stake in improving services for disabled children, although this carries the risk that they will opt for highly visible options such as buildings which can be opened and which will remain as a monument to their beneficence!

Sadly, I suspect the main reason for poor service in most agencies is apathy, which puts disabled children so far down the priority list that not many people really care. Apathy, or alienation, has been generated in many social work agencies by a continuing bombardment of unrealistic expectations, meaningless bureaucratic demands and perceived lack of value from political masters. Neither social work, nor its clients, matter much to wider society. There has been little protest about the state of service provision for disabled children and little incentive for change. This state of affairs devalues disabled children and, by association, diminishes all of us.

Organisational structures: the options for change

While it is hard to detect much fundamental change from grassroots level, recent legislation and right-wing ideological pressures have created organisational changes which are politically driven and management led. The most fundamental of these has been the introduction into local authorities of the internal market, or the purchaser/provider split. This is based on the theory that by separating the purchasing of service from its provision, a more effective distribution system will emerge since providers will no longer be assessing for their own service and perhaps pushing it unfairly. As a concept, it has worked best for adult services, where the assessment could be envisaged as a 'care management' role, which would then access a budget to purchase services such as residential care. Care management, despite the emphasis in the NHS and Community Care Act for assessment to be needs led, is a system in danger of becoming assessment for services already supplied. The fundamental issue of whether the care manager, or any purchaser, is responsible to their employer or to their client is as yet unresolved. It is an old issue about the clear responsibilities of professionals versus the requirements of employers which often seem deliberately ambiguous. Underlying this is the question of whether care management should be envisaged as a competency-based, bureaucratic function or as a professional activity involving ethical judgement.

Professionalism has been in retreat from new managerialism for some years, and both the National Health Service and latterly local authorities have begun to acquire a pseudo-business language and culture, reflected by new titles such as 'executives', 'care managers' and 'business units'. The purchaser/provider split propagates the myth that welfare services can be bought and sold like goods in a street market, and that the best stallholders will thrive as the shopping public patronises their stalls and deserts the inefficient and sub-standard.

This reliance on market forces to achieve efficiency is a basic precept of the Conservative government but even in the real marketplace it has fundamental flaws which are even more apparent when applied to welfare services. It makes assumptions about the ability of customers or service users to select the best product which take no account of such issues as the persuasiveness of advertising, the variable quality of information and its accessibility, the conditions under which such decisions may have to be made or the reliability of advice available. An individual in need of help may have poor information about options, be feeling ill or under stress, be under pressure to leave a hospital or to accept a service presented by a pushy salesperson. The market is driven by a need to maximise profits rather than be effective for the customer. It follows that persuading people to pay more for less content is better for the grocer. Such an ethos does not translate comfortably into social welfare. Local authorities are expected to demonstrate equity in service delivery which is not compatible with the free for all of the marketplace in which customers who are less able to push to the front get served last and take what is left.

Myths about what constitutes quality service are being reinforced by the jargon about customer care and the high profile given to charters, despite few 'customers' being involved in standard setting. There is clearly a political dimension here, from the ideological pressure to create a self-sufficient, purchasing society in a free market to local political agendas which are variously compliant or resistant to such changes.

A role for the social worker as a provider of service, such as advocacy or counselling, has been easy to eliminate from the picture, especially as it had not existed for many adults beforehand. Social work visits may have been therapeutic, but they were never sold as such, and few assessments cite 'social work' as a need, nor cost it.

The picture in children's services is different, and many childcare divisions have resisted the pressure to adopt a purchaser/provider split as the NHS and Community Care Act is seen somehow to relate only to adults. Some that have adopted the model are now reconsidering their position. The SSI are also currently undertaking work on appropriate organisational structures for childcare agencies. It proved hard organisationally to restructure along two lines at once, and the internal market has touched all sectors, but childcare social workers are envisaged as directly delivering service, and this different concept of their role has created internal markets which are not so pure in their division, and enabled much of childcare work to retain a role which does not fit so neatly the marketplace ideology. Childcare workers are consequently still more likely than their counterparts in adult services both to assess a need for and to deliver a service. This reflects some of the fudging around the purchaser/provider split which left much medical decision-making intact in the Health Service, where a surgeon will still both diagnose and also do the cutting. Despite the rhetoric, and despite being longer into the business culture, professional decision-making in the Health Service did not experience the same insults to professional integrity under the ideology of purchaser/provider split which some local authority workers encountered.

Although the Health Service was divided organisationally into purchasing health authorities and provider trusts, there was not the same degree of organisational change experienced by some right-wing local authorities where directly provided services such as old people's homes and home care services were sold off to the private sector in overnight demonstrations of ideological fervour. Healthcare trusts remain part of the National Health Service. In such local authorities, work with adults is reduced to the operation of bureaucratic procedures and the application of preset criteria, while performance is measured by throughput. This is scarcely to be conceptualised as social work, or as a professional task at all, and will undoubtedly become the province of unqualified, inexpensive staff who are less likely to question the value or the sense of the activity in which they are engaged. This is better news for auditors than it is for vulnerable people.

While childcare services have been able to some extent to resist the worst excesses of the marketplace ideology, this has been harder in relation to disabled children. Existing services for disabled children fit more neatly into the adult conceptualisation of service pattern than that for children, and many were traditionally managed as adjuncts of adult services. Disabled children were seen as disabled first, and social work can easily be marginalised as a service in its own right, since there has been, and sometimes still is, a tendency to assess for and recommend routinised, off-the-shelf solutions such as respite.

There are some detectable moves to introduce the concept of needs-led assessments within a purchaser/provider model. If conducted with a genuinely open mind, a needs-led assessment is certainly an improvement on an assessment conducted for a predetermined service, but it does not offer any fundamental challenge to the concept that assessment can be split off as a separate role from that of providing help. In other words the assessor does not expect to provide any service in person.

In one urban authority, where the purchaser/provider split runs up to director level, assessments previously done by providers are now done by a team of assessors. Following assessment, providers are asked to set up services on a competitive basis and according to a time-limited business contract, within a business culture. Only child protection remains as a collaborative venture. Social workers have vanished from the scene altogether as their role has split into a range of functionary tasks.

Social work with disabled children fits neatly into the same broker role that has been the fate of social work with adults and in many cases has suffered the same fate: social workers were replaced by care managers. Children are regarded as problem cases that need to be placed within an appropriate service slot. Since efficiency is measured by throughput, speed is of the essence. As long as managers are themselves assessed on performance indicators which relate solely to numbers, children are in danger of being treated as commodities to be shifted along a conveyer: assess, place, NFA, next case please! Disabled children are at particular risk of being objectified in this way.

The education world has tried to counter the worst excesses of league tables by introducing the concept of value added, which would give credit for *improvements* in educational standards which respected different starting-points. In other words a position at the top of the league is easy if the students come from advantaged backgrounds and are intelligent, but improving the skills of a child from a disadvantaged home, or who is less academic, indicates better teaching. This concept has been resisted as harder to measure and both the popular press and the advantaged schools and universities much prefer the simplistic league system based on exam results. Nonetheless, value added is a concept which has more merit in terms of assessing quality of education. Social services need to develop similar indicators to offset the pressure to measure by client contacts, cases opened or children placed on registers. In the case of disabled children, the number successfully included in mainstream provisions would be a nice start!

There is a growing recognition in some areas that disabled children are children, and should receive services within a childcare framework. Where local authorities have decided to provide for disabled children, the purchaser/provider decision has been made in conjunction with two more basic decisions. First whether services for disabled children should be managed as part of children's services and, if so, whether to opt for specialist or integrated teams. These decisions are made within a wider environment of cultural change, where the managerial ethos of the marketplace is affecting other services such as health and education.

Specialism v. integration

In discussions about services for disabled children, the question usually arises of whether or not specialist teams are the best way forward. There is not a straightforward answer to this. Parents may prefer a specialist team if they see it as representing expertise and commitment. It seems to me that the attitude and values of the team, and the resources and information to which they have access are more important to the service user than the structure of the organisation. It is also important not to confuse the status of the team with the sort of services they are recommending. If, for example, a specialist team is also recommending specialist services as a matter of routine, it is clearly a force for the continued marginalisation of disabled children. On the other hand, if it consists of people making genuine efforts to find ways to access mainstream provisions by helping mainstream providers to adapt to including disabled clients, it is a positive force, and it may be that members of a specialist team have more time to undertake such advocacy work. There is an obvious need for specialist teams to have clearly stated aims and objectives. These could link with performance indicators that have some real value, such as getting service providers to accept disabled children and make appropriate arrangements for their full inclusion.

There are several commonly made arguments in favour of specialism, some of which hold more currency than others. It is perhaps wise to be aware of the vested interests of those making recommendations before reaching any decisions as to the worth of the argument itself. One centres on the expertise of the team members, and their consequent ability to form professional relationships with medical personnel. This is a poor argument. Any competent social worker can form a relationship with a medical practitioner, and does not need to learn to speak Latin or Greek to do so. The 'handmaiden' approach that some medical social workers used to adopt toward consultants is not only dated but leaves the consultant to set the agenda. Disability is not an illness and a medically led agenda is inappropriate. Many consultant paediatricians nowadays are trying to adopt a partnership approach, which means that social workers respond by being much more confident about their own roles.

A second argument, which has more practical worth, centres on the knowledge and experience that the team members build up in a particular service area. This involves understanding the interdisciplinary links and being able to work across agency boundaries. There is nothing very different in this from other childcare work, except that the individuals and institutions across the fences will be different, given that social security, education and health services also segregate disabled children. This knowledge of other agencies extends to knowledge of technical equipment around disability or skills in using a sign language.

This argument also rests on a pragmatic understanding that social workers may not stay in their jobs long enough to learn a genuinely generic role. The counter argument to this is that it can perpetuate a segregated system, and absolve the rest of the social workers in the authority from including disabled children in their thinking. The plea of most workers that they cannot work with disabled children because they cannot communicate is often made and is a thin disguise for disablism.

This 'out of sight, out of mind' approach of organisations to disability is pernicious and damaging without actually being overtly hostile. It ensures no progress is ever made down the main line by steering disability issues into a siding.

A third argument is purely pragmatic and one with which I confess to having considerable sympathy, at least at grassroots level. This simply states that specialist teams are not the alternative to integrated teams, but to no service at all. This argument is made by those who believe that integration is preferable, but cannot hope that their authority would provide sufficient resources to ensure that disabled children got a look in within integrated teams where they were competing with child protection cases. (These kind of arguments usually talk of disability work and child protection as if they are mutually exclusive, which is sometimes a self-fulfilling prophecy.)

A development from the above argues that the specialist team is simply a stepping stone on the way to integration: that having raised the profile of disabled children, and established a basis of need and a pattern of service provision, the team can later become an integral part of the mainstream childcare services. This is a highly theoretical argument. In practice, where a team does provide an integrated service, this is often by one member who has a specialist brief or personal interest in the area of disability. Such individuals take on the disability cases on behalf of the team. They tend to become isolated from their teams and establish support links elsewhere, reinforcing the same pattern of absolving most childcare workers from thinking about disability that specialist teams can create.

Members of specialist teams have also reported feeling isolated from the departments they work within and from childcare teams. This sense of isolation, like loneliness, derives not from a sense of being special, but from a sense of marginalisation as a low priority service. This impression persists even when such teams are relatively well resourced in budgetary and staff terms, and despite their having considerable quality time to allocate to service users. It rests on a sense of being peripheral to the real aims of the department and of dealing with work that no one else really wants, or considers important. In this respect, the disablism of society at large is reflected in the social services department.

It follows that the value of a specialist team will depend on its own attitude towards itself and its clients. Clearly it should be child-centred and operate on the basis of placing the child's interests at the heart of its operation. More than that, it should consciously adopt a conceptual framework which sees the 'specialist' function as acting to compensate for the oppressive marginalisation which disabled children experience. That is, it exists to counter the abnormality of society which creates a marginalised situation for disabled children. This is quite different to a belief that a specialist team is necessary because the child has special needs. The problem is not the child, but the way they are treated. This may be asking for some convoluted thinking. Certainly it is different from the usual conceptualisation of a specialist team, which normally exists because a client group is seen as particularly difficult to work with. I would suggest, nonetheless, that if the conceptual jump is impossible, the team would be better integrated into a generic childcare one.

Complaints procedures

Complaints procedures serve organisations by steering people into systems which focus on individual difficulty, and rarely challenge the service on a collective basis. They are usually time consuming, and controlled by the organisation, which investigates itself. The standards against which the organisation measures itself are also self-imposed and the endemic range of charters which now exist in all areas of our lives are rarely constructed after consultation with potential users. This does not necessarily mean that the objectives are bad, but it does leave the setting of priorities with the service deliverer, not the recipient. I may prefer, for example, that my dustbin is emptied a little less often, but that the contents all reach the back of the dustbin cart rather than being scattered in the street. The most vital ingredients in the charter may be the most likely to be fudged.

A Charter example currently in my possession pledges to answer '95 per cent of all incoming calls within 3 rings, and the rest as promptly as we can'. This 95 per cent helpful beginning is ruined by the next line which undertakes: *'where appropriate, to supply what help and assistance we can'*.

Complaints procedures not only divert people from making their complaints in their own way, but can also massively divert resources. Many complaints stem from the failure to listen properly or to explain things adequately in the first place. The lengthy procedures involved in first and second stages of appeal, the involvement of panels and committees, all command resources that could arguably be better used to get things right in the first place. If organisations learn from their mistakes, complaints procedures may be justified. All too often, however, they are an alternative to fundamental change.

Resistance to change

In attempting to disentangle these threads, it has to be accepted that organisations may not actually want to change in any fundamental way. Any large organisation will have vested interests where real change is more of a threat than an opportunity and not to be risked lightly. There are numerous ways in which organisations can give the appearance of activity without actually altering anything much in reality and social services departments seem locked into many of these.

Restructuring has already been mentioned. This can involve major upheaval, and a redistribution of personnel, responsibility and lines of accountability, but still leave service provision working along much the same lines as before. Other devices involve seeking more and more information, the construction of endless reports, working parties, sub groups, pilot studies which have to be monitored and evaluated and consultation exercises: all such delaying devices are insidious because they appear constructive and, of course, when used properly, they can be constructive. It is difficult to oppose a 'consultation' exercise and demand action, even though action is precisely what is needed. The responses to my questionnaire highlighted examples of unproductive activity:

> *'Our management are not able to face the issues. We have had a working party for over 3 years making recommendations which fall into a big black hole.'*
>
> *'X County has undertaken a trawl of parents needs via parents forums – unfortunately no one seems to know what the results are, and we are about to start another.'*
>
> *'X City SSD Management are still at the stage of:*
>
> *1) dragging their feet;*
> *2) no new initiatives;*
> *3) maintaining resource led services;*
> *4) waiting for a new Director.*

Organisations not wanting to change because of fear or vested interest can be viewed either as creating obstacles intentionally or accidentally. The sinister view maintains that it is in the interests of organisations who see change as damaging or costly to reinforce the conceptual view of disabled children as pathological, deviant or the proper province of charity. Training programmes which promote a social model or universal theory are not encouraged. It is common practice to invite consultant community paediatricians to set the tone for social work training about work with disabled children and in the author's experience they rarely stick to medical matters.

Given that the maintenance of disabilist attitudes is in the interests of organisations which seek to maintain a status quo, it is worth challenging those whose development seems stuck, to find out whether this is genuine inability to see a way forward, or a more deliberate choice to sabotage progress.

The lack of a consistent purpose and theoretical framework is allowing, if not encouraging, service development that is at best piecemeal and sometimes cosmetic. This sad state of affairs is facilitated by the continuing sense of lack of worth among the target group, which has not developed any sustained protest about the quality of service. Individual parents may 'fight' for the rights of their child, but they fight within the existing structures, rather than seek to change them. There has yet to develop much consistent sense of a mass movement for change to the underlying philosophy of childhood disability as individual pathology and need. It is probably from there that any challenge has to develop.

Effective challenge to inert organisations, whether from within or externally, is more likely to be on a collective rather than on an individual basis, and organisations resistant to change are more fearful of such activity. Advocacy organisations may find difficulty in securing funding from local authorities on the pretext that they are 'lobbying', which is a political activity, rather than representing which is an activity promoted by the Department of Health that local authorities are expected to encourage.

Local authority fears will not be the official explanation of resistance to groupwork or community action by social workers, who can make powerful alliances with service users when knowledge is shared. Despite the principles of the Children Act, real partnership between professional and service user is not attractive to the new management, nor to the legal functionaries who serve it. Social workers from a number of authorities have reported being actively discouraged by their managers from groupwork activity, which is conducted in their own time as a semi-legitimate activity and not counted as part of their official workload. The increasing emphasis of new managerialism on counting, measuring and relating pay to performance is designed to discourage these kinds of extra-curriculum activities. Such work is designated low or no priority, not because it is a waste of time for the service user or professional, but because it threatens the smooth running of the bureaucratic machine.

An effective challenge for disabled children would therefore need to combine a shift in attitude from individual pathology toward an understanding of institutional discrimination, and away from individual casework toward collective action. It should focus not on extending the range of segregated services, but on challenging the barriers to mainstream services that exclude disabled children.

This means social workers being prepared to share their power: the knowledge of and access to the system. It also means parents being prepared to work for all disabled children, rather than to fight just for special treatment for their own child.

Conclusion

All this seems to bring us a long way from the Children Act, with its new duties to promote and ensure the welfare of children and minimise the effects of disability. What is happening in practice is that a combination of loosely worded legislation, resistance to change and deeply disabilist organisations are combining to render ineffective the legislation as it relates to disabled children.

The bottom line is that the powerful counterbalances that have always oppressed disabled children are still in place and still being allowed to operate, despite the very genuine efforts of some committed individuals. Post Children Act, disabled children are still being marginalised albeit within new structures and by a different set of workers.

Although any improvements are helpful in themselves, real change can only occur if there is a fundamental shift in approach away from a medical model of service provision, which pathologises the child and victimises its parents, towards a social model which sees disabled children as oppressed, devalued and marginalised by society. This is no longer a case therefore of just nudging the wheels. There is room for intervention into the vicious circle of oppression at all stages in the life cycle, by both disabled and non-disabled adults. Victories within the adult disability movement will help, since a greater respect for disabled adults will engender a greater emphasis on developing disabled children as future citizens, not future dependants. Parents are a disabled child's best hope of developing a positive self-image and changes should be sought in health, education and social welfare provision which recognise a child's rights as well as their needs. Service providers have a responsibility, at whatever level, to challenge existing practices which offer 'help' while destroying self-esteem, splitting families, ignoring race and reinforcing disability as a route for oppressive practices.

These are not just matters for individual social workers but for councils, social services management, professional bodies and trade unions. All the same it remains the case that individual social workers must attempt to influence these organisations from their perspective as practitioners.

The final section in this book focuses more closely on the role of the individual social worker in challenging current practice and making changes. It would be wrong to pretend this is easy. Social work with disabled children operates within a culture which actively discriminates, and which is capable of making a conceptual distinction between 'disabled children' and 'children' which excludes the former group. Disabled children are children who are different from the majority, and they are oppressed by reason of this difference. Before exploring ways in which social work can make a positive difference, the next two chapters explore this cultural context, and attempt an understanding of what it is like growing up in a society which places a low value on your life.

Chapter 2:
To Be or Not To Be?

'My daughter has Down's syndrome. It is the most painful thing I will ever say but my wife and I wish she had had a test. If she had we would have terminated the pregnancy' Simon Walters, Political Editor, *The Sun.* Quoted in *The Observer* 16 July 1995

> In 'The Masterpiece Society' the voyagers of the Starship Enterprise boldly go to a human colony where genetic engineering has been in force for the last 200 years. Not only are unwanted characteristics screened out, but colonists are genetically preprogrammed to fulfil roles in society. *No need to anguish over what you want to be when you grow up!* Commander Geordi la Forge, chief engineer of the Enterprise, whose skills are called upon to save the colony from certain destruction, from a passing stellar core, faces the unpalatable fact that had he been conceived there he would not have been permitted to be born. Geordi is blind.
>
> The scientist from the colony explains to Geordi that he would have been terminated as a cell because 'it was the wish of our founders no one should have to suffer disabilities'
>
> Geordi replies: *'Who gave them the right to decide whether I should be here; whether or not I might have something to contribute?'*

On 16 February 1995 Granada Television screened a programme in their 3-D series entitled 'Licence to Kill?' which asked the question: 'Should parents be allowed to decide the fate of their newborn child or should doctors have a licence to kill?' This somewhat sensational choice was the opener to a programme which dealt with the dilemmas facing parents and doctors when children are born with severe disability. The programme pointed out that Dutch doctors are allowed to kill babies provided they stick to proper guidelines, but here in Britain such 'mercy killings' are performed in secret, and often without the knowledge of parents. A Dutch doctor, Zier Versluys, defended his position:

> *'I don't think at all that a doctor should always preserve life. A doctor should preserve life as long as life is something good for the patient. I think in these exceptional circumstances death has more value than life and helping a baby to die is not wrong.'*

British medical opinion is divided. John Wyatt, a paediatrician rightly raised the question of whether either the doctor or the parent had the right to decide. Richard Nicholson, on the other hand, admitted to killing babies by slowly raising the dose of painkillers until the child became comatose and gently let go of life. He made it sound quite nice. His justification for bringing about the death of disabled babies also rested on his wish to relieve the suffering of nursing staff and parents.

Parental views were also mixed. Stephanie Harrell, who is anencephalic (born with neither brain nor scalp), is kept alive by medical science following a court injunction taken out by her mother, a committed Christian who is waiting for a miracle. The mother of Dominic Kennedy, a four year old with cerebral palsy, while confessing that *'it is very hard to make the decision to deny the chance to life to a child that you've given birth to,'* nonetheless believes that *'I think it would have been in his best interests to end his life because he has no real future.'* She believes the decision belongs to the parents, not the doctors, because it is they who have to take the child home and care for it, a caring that for disabled children *'goes on and on'*. It is the parents, in other words, who have to manage the consequences of the medical decision. These children clearly have very different degrees of disability. Stephanie has never been viable without life support and active medical intervention and arguably has never been 'alive' in the sense of having any consciousness. Dominic, despite his mother's assertion that the only meaning in his life is that given to him by his family, appeared a happy child, and his death would require killing him, not the withdrawal of life support, as with Stephanie. There are clearly very different moral issues here, but the attitudes of the parents also tells us a great deal about different reactions to caring for a dependent child.

On 14 March 1995 the BBC screened a programme which told the story of Helen Pusey, 'one of the first women in Britain to benefit from test tube fertility treatment' (*The Guardian,* 14.3.95). Helen had four eggs fertilised and rejected the offer to kill two in the womb to give the other two a better chance. Two of the quads subsequently died shortly after a three months premature birth by Caesarean section. The other two are disabled, one at six years old still needing to be tube fed directly to his stomach. Helen's fifth child was conceived normally, making the bitterly ironic point that the previous medical intervention was not only highly risky but unnecessary.

I have dwelt on these programmes because they illustrate a number of pertinent, controversial and painful issues.

The 3-D programme featured a number of people, doctors and parents advocating the killing of disabled children. Both cerebral palsy and hydrocephalus were mentioned as conditions which might attract this fate. Despite this frightening message the programme was screened at peak family viewing time: 7.30 in the evening, when children with cerebral palsy might well have been watching. No one would dream of screening a programme advocating the killing of red-haired children at such a time of day. This insensitivity serves to underline the fact that the feelings of disabled children who might be watching were not considered, and reinforces the notion that it is possible to conceptualise disabled children as a separate group: not really counting as *children* at all. If their sensitivity and feelings are denied, it is that much easier to consider them as 'non-beings' and therefore easier to kill.

Second, there is an issue of *who* decides which lives are worth living. The evidence is that, left to either doctors or parents, the chance of survival has become a lottery which bears little relationship to actual level of pain, impairment or the viability of life without artificial support. Geordi la Forge is quite clear no one but himself has the right to rule on that one, but what about newly born infants? In China the eugenics programme, with its emphasis on quality rather than quantity, has condemned huge numbers of disabled children to 'orphanages', often to die.

Third, there is the issue of responsibility for care. This is closely related to the second issue, since the belief that one might be faced with a long, difficult and lonely caring task is certain to affect a decision about whether or not to abort, allow a baby to die, or have it killed.

This also raises questions about parental expectations of children and the level of care that parents should reasonably expect to provide when they decide to raise a family. Is the extra care required when a child is disabled part of the normal range of what is reasonable within a family, or should some children attract extra state help?

Fourth, the programmes raise many sticky issues around the value and ethics of medical intervention or experimentation. Advances in medical science mean that many children survive nowadays who might otherwise have died, but there are costs. Children born with impairments represent failures of medical science, but as with the Pusey children they can also represent the results of medical experimentation. Other children are born with impairments as a result of the poor health or maternal care of the mother, or more avoidable abuse such as smoking while pregnant. Disability in infants is therefore often a creation of society, rather than an act of God, and this should be the basis from which society starts its thinking about its obligations toward those children whom it has failed. Unfortunately this is seldom the case: there is a marked reluctance to accept that such children deserve compensation for the disadvantage they are born with. Indeed, discrimination is likely to continue: a double insult.

Eugenics, then, is not simply a matter for science fiction nor for the third world. We may jibe in this rich country at tales from India about abortions of female children, but the same process occurs where we seek to eliminate certain medical or disabling conditions by screening. The message this sends out about the value of the life of a child with, say, Down's syndrome, is essentially the same message as the one given by those who abort female foetuses in India: they do not matter. Disabled children are denied the same right to life as their able bodied contemporaries.

The Abortion Act of 1967 makes termination possible if there 'is a substantial risk that if the child were born it would suffer from such physical or mental abnormalities as to be seriously handicapped' Such terms as *substantial, risk, suffer* and *serious* are not defined, and the decision is left very much to the doctors. Identifying unacceptable differences before birth and then aborting the foetus is a potentially highly dangerous by-product of genetic engineering (Hilary Rose 1994). The press excitement about the discovery of the 'gay gene' conveyed a similar message about homosexual people in its attempt to eliminate deviance by disposing of those who do not fit the definition of normality.

Abortion is legal up to the moment of birth for children with serious handicaps, the definition of which is still in the hands of the medical profession. The discrimination against foetuses diagnosed as disabled, or potentially so, is quite clear, and still successfully defended on grounds both related to the anticipated cost of care and assumptions made (usually by doctors) about the anticipated quality of life of the child. It is becoming increasingly clear that such discrimination continues beyond birth and that disabled babies are at risk of being killed by doctors, with or without the consent of parents, who assess their lives as not worth living, or the amount of care they would require as being unacceptably high. Helen Pusey agreed to ending the life of one of her children, whose impairment seemed particularly severe, in order to devote resources to the two who were less damaged. The pressure on parents facing such decisions is enormous.

Even after birth, the power of the medical profession continues to be quite disproportionate in the lives of many disabled children. Having no means to cure, consultants instead adopt roles such as educational advisor or family therapist in a way that would be quite unacceptable to parents whose children were not disabled. I once attended a conference at which a consultant paediatrician, having admitted he could only diagnose the cause of disability in half the children he saw and had no cure for any of them, then went on to describe case studies for the next half hour centred on the advice he had given to parents about their child's schooling. I finally gave way to my anger when he talked of a child with a degenerative condition, for whom he had recommended mainstream education until he needed a wheelchair, after which he would have to transfer to special school. It is tempting to name this young doctor, particularly as he ignored the letter I wrote to him subsequently, but I suspect he is only typical of his breed. That paediatricians feel able to offer *educational* advice is bad enough: that it is of such poor quality adds insult to injury. What is infinitely worse is that parents may give it credibility.

The idea that you do not argue with the doctor is very powerful conditioning. This disproportionate influence seems likely to continue for as long as disability is confused with ill health and medical science is credited with more accuracy than it really has. The confusion of disability and ill health is deeply ingrained in our thinking, even at the highest levels. The fact that the census could ask people to return a **yes/no** to the question 'Are you chronically sick or disabled?' is evidence of such muddled thinking. Doctors are all too frequently credited with diagnostic, prognostic and intervention skills far in excess of their actual ability. This is partly the wish of patients to *believe*, but also of doctors to continue to make a mystique of their profession. All too often treatment is a matter of seeing what will work, and prognosis is a best guess. Many parents of disabled children will report that they received early prognoses from doctors which turned out to be unduly negative. While the better than predicted progress of the child is often attributed to efforts on behalf of parents, portage or physiotherapy, the chances are that it was the prediction itself which was wrong. Nonetheless, as a society, we continue to demonstrate great faith in the infallibility of the medical profession, even down to influencing decisions about whether or not to continue with a pregnancy.

I struggle, as I am sure many readers will, with reconciling the right of a woman to choose to carry a child, or not, with the right of a disabled child to the same chance of being born as one without any known impairment. In arguing for the right of the child I find myself in danger of being perceived as allied with anti-abortion groups, but this is not an argument against a women's right to choose abortion. Nonetheless, and however uncomfortable it may feel, we have to recognise the issue as an act of discrimination against certain children, and think about the negative message to disabled children about themselves, about their place in society, and their value in other people's eyes, if the very fact of *risk* of impairment is a death sentence. Jenny Morris, who also recognised a personal conflict about the rights of women and the rights of disabled children, writes very fully about the issues surrounding abortion (Morris 1991).

Discriminatory abortion rules have an impact on the self-esteem of disabled children and adults who are allowed to live or who slip through the screening net. In addition they have a pernicious effect by feeding the disabilist attitudinal set of the whole society. Discriminatory abortion sets a baseline on the value of life that is *less* for a 'disabled' child than for one who is 'normal' (and we can debate both definitions). This makes it less likely that we can achieve any ambitions for disabled children to become accepted as equal members of society. If the foundations are not level, the building is likely to tilt. This sense of being of less value can be internalised by disabled children. It is likely to be reinforced by insensitive remarks made to child or mother which almost any child born with a disability can report, such as 'If it was mine, I'd put a pillow over its head'.

The devaluation of the life of a disabled child is reinforced at birth by the medical and paramedical professions who 'break' the news, separate the mother from those who have given birth to a 'normal' child, and offer genetic counselling to avoid any repetition of the 'tragedy'. The language used is instructive.

The reaction to the death of a disabled child is also often different and equally devaluing. Parents may well feel denied full permission to grieve by comments such as 'well, it was a blessing, really'.

It is clear that as a society we do not want to include disabled children. We do our best to prevent their birth. If this fails we seek to 'normalise' them. If this fails we render them invisible by an elaborate system of segregation.

Attempts to normalise the child mean getting it to look and behave as near to the standard able-bodied model as possible. A range of techniques are available to eliminate the difference and squeeze the child by fair means or foul into an acceptable format. Down's children can get their faces rearranged to fit the standard pattern. Children are forced to adopt painful and inefficient walking patterns rather than use wheelchairs, not because of a reasoned choice about the most effective and least painful method of mobility, but because using a wheelchair is stigmatic and a powerful symbol of dependency. Children without limbs are squeezed into artificial arms and legs which imitate the missing limbs. Thalidomide children were terrified by attempts to re-create the limbs they were missing, because it was so hard for the rest of us to accept children without limbs. Children are strapped upright for hours in metal frames rather than being allowed to stay on the floor. All these devices are designed to make the children look normal, rather than to maximise the use of their own bodies, or achieve the most efficient dexterity or mobility. Some deaf children are still denied the advantage of Sign Language. Conductive *education* as a system for developing motor skills in children with cerebral palsy and similar conditions has received extensive publicity and attracted considerable fund raising, which appeal to parental wishes to normalise their children by actively doing something. Even if it was desirable to concentrate so much effort on a single aspect of a child's growth and development, the hard evidence is that conductive education makes no significant long-term difference to children's progress. (Barstow et al 1993) Its popularity is not based on facts, but on the desire of parents to normalise their children in a society which they know will actively discriminate against them if they fail to fit the standard pattern. In that quest, wider considerations and long-term consequences are often lost. Nonetheless, the popularity of conductive education does beg some questions about the educational system currently available. This is discussed later.

All these efforts to make a child normal by stimulating brain waves, hanging them upside down, pushing, pulling and cajoling, mean that the child receives the very clear message that there is something about them that nobody likes. Chances are that they will learn not to like it either. Since it is likely to be something about which, realistically, they can do little or nothing, this overemphasis is likely only to create a sense of failure or even of self-hate.

In seeking to eliminate difference, and produce all children to the same specification, we can create in the child a deep and lasting inferiority complex. This pain can persist throughout an adulthood of deference to non-disabled people, and even to those disabled in adulthood, who have not experienced the destructive negative socialisation of a disabling childhood.

The early hours, days and years of disabled children are often characterised by separation for medical or social reasons from the mother, at the same time as she is being treated differently from those who have given birth to children who are 'all right'. In the meantime, the father is probably having a man-to-man chat with the consultant and keeping his cigars firmly in his pocket, while friends are not sure whether to congratulate or commiserate. Exploring the knock-on effects of the parents' treatment in reinforcing feelings of failure or inadequacy leads us into even deeper waters. Do they hold the baby in quite the same way? Do they transmit any of their disappointment, guilt, pain or confusion? Does the baby pick up any of the ambivalence and conflict its parents may be experiencing? We do not know!

The effects of the physical and emotional separation of mother and child so early in life have never been thoroughly researched, but we do know enough about bonding (building a relationship) to know that it is an unhealthy process. A poor relationship with a child is one of the factors which increases risk of abuse.

Yet this has been relegated or disregarded altogether in the early care of disabled children where the importance of medical intervention and/or hospitalisation to tackle the physical impairment can take an easy precedence. What needs more closely questioning is the weight in the decision-making process given to the effects of separation against the particular medical intervention or perceived social need under consideration. Serious questions also need asking about the increased likelihood of experimental medical techniques being used on children who have impairments, particularly where these are painful and carry little chance of success.

None of the above is intended to deny the right of disabled children to medical treatment, but to plead for a more thoughtful separation of those interventions to counter ill health, those which counter disabling conditions, those which are broadly cosmetic, and those which are for academic research.

Indeed, disabled children may be at risk of not receiving adequate medical treatment for ill health. There is risk of a failure to recognise conditions because of the tendency to attribute things that seem wrong to the disability, and a disabled child may be given lower priority for treatment. These discriminations also apply to dental treatment.

This may be compounded for black children, given that black communities as a whole enjoy a lower standard of medical care than the population at large

(Torkington 1991). This is compounded for black people by poverty, poorer housing and higher unemployment. It is arguable that more disability is created within black communities in the first place.

Disabled children are exposed constantly to images of themselves as second best, pathetic objects of charity, problems, and disappointments to their parents. Too much emphasis on therapy to put things right denies the right of children to be valued for themselves. When too much emphasis is placed on one factor, such as walking or talking, the price of failure is enormous because children may internalise the belief of being permanent failures. Such negative views of self not only hinder aspirations for themselves, but prevent them recognising the value of other disabled children and adults as advisers, advocates or role models.

Education

> *'The diagnosis they were given was cerebral palsy but I never realised that I had a disability until I left school. You don't realise that you're not going to get a lift everywhere – when you're at residential school you get a bus everywhere. I didn't realise I was different until I was 16.'*
>
> Terry, quoted in Morris (1995)

When it refers to services for disabled children, 'special' is a euphemism. Special education is a system designed to keep disabled children out of the sight of 'normal' children, often by long daily journeys from home, or even by the use of residential facilities. Establishments which euphemistically offer a school year of 52 weeks are very thinly disguised segregated institutional care. Jenny Morris's recent research for the Who Cares Trust is sharply critical of poor standards in residential care. (Morris 1995). Special education flies in the face of sound childcare and educational principles by accepting lower standards than mainstream education, dampening expectations, and destroying aspirations. It teaches social inferiority. However enlightened the curriculum of a particular school may be, children leaving it are likely to feel different, uncomfortable and abnormal. Despite the arguments against special education being won over a decade ago, and the right to non-segregated education being enshrined in law, the 1981 Education Act has still exposed many disabled children to the damaging process of growing up in an environment where they are, by definition, second class. The 1993 Education Act has not altered this fundamental discrimination.

Disabled children are rarely consulted about their own education, but there is a growing wealth of evidence from disabled writers which confirms the problems inherent within the educational system, albeit often in retrospect. There is nothing odd in this: most of us can only assess the value of our own education afterwards, and from meeting contemporaries whose experiences have been very different. At the time, most children are likely only to be conscious of their happiness, whether they like the teachers or not, and whether they are achieving according to the expectations of the school and their parents. A number of the women writing in Lois Keith's *Mustn't Grumble* refer to the inadequacy of their education. Nasa Begum perhaps gives the most balanced view, reflecting both the childhood pleasure of the bus trip and the later realisations of being cheated:

> *My 'real' school, the school that was different from the one my sisters went to, catered for children with physical disabilities from nursery school right up to the age of sixteen. We were all transported to and from school in single decker buses as children came there from all over the city. For some of us, by the time we arrived in school we had already been travelling for over an hour. The bus journey was one of the best parts of the school day because the activities we had started in the playground would extend into our journey to and from school. You could make or break friends, play games and share gossip. I used to enjoy waiting on the pavement each morning, there seemed to be something special about being collected for school from my own doorstep... I didn't do as much academic work as my sisters in mainstream schools, and one of the reasons for this was the bane of my life – physiotherapy. I was sure I was treated unjustly as not everyone in class had to go away to these sessions and, what was worse, it didn't even exist in my sisters' school. I couldn't see the point of all these agonising exercises. I was never very good at accepting the fact that things I didn't like could be 'good for me' and the physiotherapist managed to do a really good job of making me a conscientious objector for the rest of my life... Looking back, I find it hard to believe that I was denied the right to have the same education as my sisters, that they went to the primary school right next to our house, while I travelled for an hour across town.*
>
> (Begum 1994: p 47-51)

There are no indications that segregated education is on the way out. New arrangements in schools which are underpinned by a marketplace philosophy and driven by examination league tables are increasing the numbers of children in special schools, despite parents wishes (The Guardian 1.9.94). The Centre for Studies on Inclusive Education (CSIE) campaigns against this trend as an erosion of human rights for disabled schoolchildren, because they are not seen as attractive commodities in the new marketplace.

Children growing up with low senses of self-esteem are less likely to contribute fully to society as adults, instead tending to see themselves as dependent and deferring to the views of the able-bodied.

In interviewing school leavers as a result of the 1986 Disabled Persons Act, social workers in Sefton MBC found that most young people had low expectations and many were unable to respond at all to enquiries about how they saw their own futures (Sefton Social Services 1990). This low self-esteem can extend to unrealistic beliefs about the wisdom and power of the unimpaired. Misunderstandings with deaf people with whom I worked some years ago were as much to do with their perception of hearing people as all powerful and therefore deliberately withholding resources as they had to do with problems inherent in trying to communicate across a language barrier.

Indoctrinating whole sections of our society with such negative views of themselves serves no one's interests in the long run and society is diminished by it. Taking a purely cost-effective stance, the Department of Employment and local authorities are preprogramming many young people into the expensive dependency of sheltered workshops, day centres and adult training centres. The depth of personal misery caused by these dehumanising processes is immeasurable.

Integration into mainstream education has not necessarily improved things, and it is probably this failure that has enabled segregated education to regain ground. The problem has centred on the reality of 'integration', which is not achievable simply by teaching disabled children in the same building. Indeed, some patterns of integrated education serve only to emphasise inadequacy and disability. The principal campaigning body for integrated education in this country, the Centre for Studies on Integration in Education, changed its name to the Centre for Studies on Inclusive Education in recognition of the need to go one better than simply ending segregation.

While not a universal phenomenon, there is evidence that substantial numbers of disabled young people lack the same confidence and self-esteem as able-bodied contemporaries, although probable causes can only be arrived at by the kind of analysis I have been attempting.

Wade and Moore, using questionnaire and sentence completion techniques, concluded that many of the students they tested had unacceptably low self-esteem. *'Many viewed their disabilities as deficits and a main reason for people disliking them.'* (Wade and Moore 1993:p161).

After reviewing a number of studies on adolescents, Hirst and Baldwin conclude, tentatively, that, while there is no consensus on the issue, disabled young people

> *'do not invariably feel inadequate and powerless... nonetheless certain broad tendencies are clear. Although some young people in the comparison group had a poor view of themselves and their abilities, disabled young people were more likely to report feelings which reflected lack of personal worth, responsibility and self determination. The more severely disabled young people were most likely to have low self esteem and limited sense of control over their lives'*
>
> (Hirst and Baldwin 1994:p65)

They go on to conclude that those at greatest risk of feeling worthless and helpless were disabled young people who had attended segregated schools and had nowhere to go.

Hirst and Baldwin argue that children attending segregated schools had generally poorer self-concepts than disabled young people from mainstream schools.

> *Although not large, the differences were statistically significant, suggesting that disabled young people from mainstream schools and colleges had a slightly more positive evaluation of themselves.*
>
> (Hirst and Baldwin 1994:p 58).

It is not possible, of course, to conclude from this that the difference was caused by the education itself, since it could reflect the kind of children or families who have the confidence or influence to use mainstream education in the first place. Nevertheless, the fact that young people do leave special education with lower self-esteem has to be a matter of concern. This was confirmed in the study by Sefton Social Services, who found disabled school leavers, by and large, were unable to formulate any aspirations for their own futures, quite contrary to initial fears on the part of service providers that asking school leavers what they wanted as opposed to needed would result in a flood of outrageous demands (Sefton Social Services 1990).

Conductive education has emerged in the last decade as a popular option for some British parents, although it has been attacked as oppressive and based on unsound ideology:

> *It is sad but understandable that the parents of disabled children should clutch at the straw of conductive education as a means of resolving their own problems. To have a handicapped child in a society which has developed a fetishism for normality and which fails to even acknowledge the needs of these parents, let alone make any provision to meet them, is clearly a profoundly disturbing experience*
>
> (Oliver 1993: p165)

In the same Open University reader, Virginia Beardshaw, a parent, takes issue with him on the grounds that conductive education provides skilled help and motivation to children whom the rehabilitation specialists in this country have written off (Beardshaw 1993). This is, of course, an argument for improving the education offered in our schools, and for re-educating teachers to motivate and raise the expectations they have of children.

These are complex matters. Parents do not chose to take their children to Hungary without weighing up the options, and it seems important to tease out what is effective about the Peto system and try to offer some of the same benefits in mainstream education here. For some parents, the attraction will be in the very fact that Peto is foreign, expensive to access and involves family sacrifice. This is not a balanced judgement in educational terms, but may reflect a need to prove good parenthood by chasing treatment which is elusive, exotic and expensive. For others, the decision may be based more objectively on the relative merits of Peto and what is on offer locally. Changing the educational opportunities here by fighting the education department may seem too slow: children grow up too fast!

No one would deny that an education system should seek to motivate, set ambitious expectations and be clear about its aims, all of which apply to the Peto Institute and all of which are common failings of special education in this country.

However, the Peto Institute is free to select its pupils and in choosing only those children whose chances of making progress are already high can demonstrate a good success rate. It is relatively easy to claim credit for children who succeed, while attributing failure either to the degree of impairment or the lack of effort on behalf of the child or parents. Many other 'rehabilitation' programmes for disabled children are offered on the same basis of organisational credit for success, while their providers can shake their heads in sorrow over the failures. There is never any need to make any promises. As children only grow up once, there is no way of providing any solid evidence of the effectiveness of the often expensive rehabilitation regime. In many ways there are echoes of Lourdes pilgrims here where cure is a miracle and its absence a matter of lack of faith. Either way, the Virgin Mary cannot lose.

Unlike the Peto, the state educational system in Britain has to provide for all children. It is deeply disturbing that it can segregate certain groups, and justify this as making the education for the majority more effective. It is an affront to human rights to contend that some children are less deserving than others. The process represents the thin end of a wedge that is unlikely to end by segregating disabled children. In treating children as a commodity to be measured on their way through the education system, all children are in danger of becoming valued only in terms of their examination performance. This is deeply dehumanising both for the child and for the teacher.

Education is important in all our lives, as a part of childhood and of adulthood, as a preparation for growing up and encountering the world, and as a vehicle for understanding it. Reducing it to a crammer for examinations involves an inestimable loss of opportunity for personal growth and development. Teaching should be about raising sights, widening horizons and motivating children and adults to explore, learn and think. This is equally true whatever the physical and intellectual character of the individual concerned may be.

If the education system is not working for disabled children, it is likely to be defective for others too. Getting it right for minority groups, in education, health or social services, means getting it right for everyone. The improvements in service access, information, openness and presentation rarely benefit only the minority group at which they are specifically aimed.

I stated at the beginning of this section that the arguments against segregated education had been won over a decade ago, with the implication that they did not need winning again. In the current climate that is clearly not the case. Some of the experiences of disabled children concerning their education have been mentioned, and I have also cited the moral and ethical issues of artificially segregating one group of children on the basis of physical or mental ability. These are negative arguments. The CSIE arguments for inclusion, which are backed by the Council for Disabled Children, are that inclusive education is a human right, good education and good social sense. They are worth repeating here.

TEN REASONS FOR INCLUSION

Human Rights

1. All children have a right to learn together.

2. Children should not be devalued or discriminated against by being excluded or sent away because of their disability or learning difficulty.

3. Children do not need to be protected from each other. Disabled adults, describing themselves as special school survivors, are now demanding an end to segregation.

4. There are no legitimate reasons to separate children for their education. Children belong together with advantages and benefits for everyone.

Good Education

5. Research shows children do better, academically and socially in integrated settings.

6. There is no teaching or care in a segregated school which cannot take place in an ordinary school.

7. Given commitment and support, inclusive education is a more efficient use of educational resources.

Good Social Sense

8. Segregation teaches children to be fearful, ignorant and breeds prejudice.

9. All children need an education that will help them develop relationships and prepare them for life in the mainstream.

10. Only inclusion has the potential to reduce fear and to build friendship, respect and understanding.

Arguments in favour of segregated education are nearly always based on a mixture of arrogance and ignorance, predicated on a worst-case scenario. Arguments for institutional respite as a substitute for adequate community services are also made on the same basis. Even if we accept, for a minute, the assertion that there are some children who will always be so badly damaged that they need to be segregated, this scarcely justifies building a whole system of segregated education around them. The cost per child in a residential school is astronomical. Costs get rapidly out of date, but it is salutary to note that the cost of one child in the residential school nearest to where I live is thirteen times higher than the cost allocated per child in a mainstream secondary school. This sum would purchase two full-time teachers or three care staff if allocated differently. The issue is not one of effective resource management, nor of sound education. Disabled children are segregated because we are afraid of them.

In a sense, those who uphold a segregated educational system do not need to make rational or research-based arguments, because they are wielding the power. Despite the provisions of legislation and the wishes of parents and disabled children to be treated as equal citizens, education authorities can get away with not planning for inclusive education because society is deeply disabilist, and does not envisage a future for disabled children as full citizens. The fight of disabled adults, whether directed specifically at education or not, to be recognised as full citizens, is therefore a crucial part of the struggle for change. When disabled adults are accepted as equal citizens, it will be harder to argue for the segregation of children.

The social work role as an advocate for children within the education system was discussed fully in *Children First* (Middleton 1992). Most of the suggestions about working with education departments still hold true, and I do not propose to repeat them here. However, the law has changed. Part Three of the Education Act 1993 updates the process for identifying and meeting children's needs for special education. Social workers are referred to the informative guide *Meeting Special Educational Needs* produced by the Centre for Studies on Inclusive Education. This is useful whether mainstream education is sought or the best deal within a special school. The Department for Education also produces its own guides.

A 'statement' is legal jargon. Essentially it is a written document outlining a child's educational needs and naming a school. It is legally binding on the education authority and it is therefore essential that parents are well advised before agreeing to its terms. The new Act is intended to make the process of statementing faster and more user friendly. Local authorities are now required to finalise the process within a maximum of six months, rather than the average time under the 1981 Education Act of fifteen months: a long time for a growing child. Assessments can be proposed by parents, schools, health or social services, are carried out by the education authority and must take the child's views into account. The LEA should also consult social services, although it is unlikely that most social services departments will institute a combined assessment. At present most seem to regard the consultation as involving nothing more than checking the child protection register. It follows that most of the advocacy work for disabled children will be undertaken by workers from voluntary agencies.

The appeals system is also new, taking power away from local authorities who previously conducted their own appeals systems using local councillors, and whose findings were only advisory. The new independent Special Educational Needs Tribunals will operate from a number of regional centres, making them physically less accessible, but also less tied to local politics. Decisions will be binding on education authorities. The danger is that the new system will be yet another money spinner for lawyers. It is clearly better all round if social workers or other advocates can work for an acceptable best deal with a local education authority and avoid getting sucked into what could be a traumatic and drawn out process.

While the goal of a high standard of education is sound, the process is set up in such a way that it carries the constant danger for the child or her advocates emphasising her need rather than concentrating their efforts more properly on the deficiencies of the education system. Similar pressures to stress the problems of the child attend those who seek to improve a family's financial position by obtaining disability benefits.

These are both manifestations of the institutional disabilism which permeates the English welfare system. Social services departments, as will be noted later, operate along the same lines: people have to establish 'need', not rights. The child's disability is emphasised rather than the deficiencies of the service provision for children who are different. The child is made to feel it is her fault for not being able-bodied, whereas the key issue is that society's institutions are organised in a discriminatory way which marginalises minority groups.

As well as more formal education, children also need opportunity and facilities for play, sports and leisure activities. Local authorities have responsibilities in all these arenas and should be looking at their policies and practices on the inclusion of disabled children. The dubious excuses about examination league tables and the disruptive influence on classes of children who are different are not available in a leisure context. Instead, disabled children will find themselves excluded from many facilities and organisations on the grounds of public safety, the inadequacies of supervision or that they are a fire hazard. All of these reasons are an avoidance of responsibility, and advocates for children have constantly not only to remind the service providers of that, but also to remind the children that the failure is not theirs for being different but society's for discriminating against them.

It is important to start taking a wider perspective. If practice and policies exclude disabled children, then this is inherently wrong in itself, since it is a denial of the right to be treated like any other child. However, if a service or facility can get itself geared up to include all children, the chances are that it will be a better facility all round. This includes making children welcome whatever their sex, race or disability. In considering the issues of discrimination and making plans to include all children, the organisation will have to address its own value base and motivation in offering any service at all. It is likely that the reasons given for exclusion are irrational excuses, ignorance or thoughtlessness, based on a learned belief that disabled children somehow matter less and have fewer rights. This kind of reasoning must be challenged at all levels, political, professional and personal.

The cultural belief that disabled children matter less feeds, and is fed by, the images which society holds about disabled children. To some extent people believe what suits them, but the availibility of information has to be a factor. Images that reinforce negative attitudes permit discriminatory actions and sustain oppression. They also send messages to disabled children that they are not wanted. The next chapter looks at some of these images.

Chapter 3
How You See Me...How You Don't

In *The Adventure of the Sussex Vampire* the Peruvian second wife of Robert Ferguson, tea broker, is accused of attacking her own baby when she is discovered with blood stained lips leaning over the child, who has a wound in his neck. She is also accused of assaulting Ferguson's first son, Jack, who is described by his father as a '*poor, little inoffensive cripple.*'

'*You would think that the dear lad's condition would soften anyone's heart*' he goes on '*A fall in childhood and a twisted spine, Mr. Holmes. But the dearest, most loving heart within.*' (p 104)

The great detective uncovers the truth. It is Jack, whose '*very soul is consumed by hatred for the splendid child, whose health and beauty are a contrast to his own weakness*' who has attacked the baby with a poisoned South American bow and arrow, having first tried out the device on the family spaniel. (p 114). Like any loving mother, Mrs. Ferguson was sucking out the poison from her baby's wound. She had chastised her step child Jack but not dared to challenge his father's view of him.

(Conan Doyle 1927, page numbers from Penguin reprint 1975)

Social workers might like to consider their approach to helping the Fergusons should they be allocated such a family: apart from the obvious move of confiscating the deadly weaponry!

It is unlikely, I hope, that such stories do much now to shape our attitudes to disabled children and such reading should do little more than make us wince at the stereotypical description which Conan Doyle got away with. The fact that most of us can find such a story quaint and out of date as a representation of disability is a sign of progress. Reading textbooks only a few years old will give similar indications. Authors of children's books, radio and television producers are showing much more awareness of their responsibilities toward disabled children. There is room for optimism, therefore, despite the continuing gruesomeness of much that is still dished up. Nonetheless, we have to ask the very serious question of how much of this represents real change of attitudes, and how much simply cosmetic changes in language.

I have chosen to start with Conan Doyle because in one short story he manages to convey three of the most enduring stereotypical images we still retain of disabled children:

> **First,** and foremost, that they are a problem, a burden to their parents, albeit through no fault of their own.
>
> **Second**, that they are objects of pity.
>
> **Third**, that disability and badness are inextricably linked and that disabled people are consumed with jealousy of able-bodied people.

Images are important because they underpin how people will behave towards disabled children, particularly in a society where they are kept hidden from most people most of the time. We behave toward strangers, by and large, in ways not based on facts and knowledge but on assumptions and stereotyping. We tend to see and experience what we expect to see and experience, if we enter situations with pre-determined ideas. Stereotyping saves time in human relationships as it precludes the need to get to know everyone as an individual by ascribing characteristics according to groups, but it is a risky strategy for those who value truth. Experiences may be atypical, or apply to a minority of situations, or be very subjective, but while they contain enough that is experienced as accurate not to disturb the stereotype in any fundamental way the images of disabled children as burdens, pitiable and a bad thing will endure.

What it is necessary to try to understand is why disabled children are sometimes experienced as burdens, what makes them targets for pity and why the link between deformity and badness persists. These understandings may help to effect change not only in imagery, but in those real experiences which serve to feed it. A disabled child can be experienced as a burden by parents for various reasons. There may be inadequate support. The parent may believe that child care should be easier. Rose tinted expectations by new parents will be disturbed by the reality of raising almost any child, but the blame for the felt hardship will centre on the disability if the firstborn has an impairment.

The emergence of the social model of disability has equipped us with a different conceptual framework for understanding that difficulties for disabled children stem not from their impairment but from the attitudes towards it and towards disabled people which are adopted by society. The problems disabled people have in negotiating life are created by other people.

It would be largely a waste of time to attempt to change the situation for disabled children by embarking on an ideological debate which seeks to claim equality of experience despite difference by denying there is any inconvenience or pain involved in disability itself. Similarly, those who advocate changing the world for disabled children by increasing their numbers belong to a fringe with whom few would identify. It is natural to want a child to be born without impairment and this is what sets the struggle for the civil rights of disabled children apart from the struggle for, say, black children: there is no inherent problem with being black. Being black is not an impairment: it is simply the response of society and its definition of power relationships which determines that black is less than equal. This response of society also applies to children with impairments but there are undeniably also very real disadvantages which are the direct results of the impairment itself. It is important to acknowledge that many of these impairments are caused by life in an unequal society

Ending racism would mean the achievement of equality between black and white people, with difference experienced as enriching and not divisive. Black and white would be represented in proportion to their numbers in all walks of life and in all kinds of employment. The current overrepresentation of black people in prison, boxing rings and poor housing would end as would their underrepresentation in the judiciary, higher education and the police force.

Ending disablism would mean an end to abortion for foetuses at risk of impairment, equality of access to health care, education, housing and shops. It would see disabled people represented in employment and in positions of power in society, and it would mean equality of respect between disabled and non-disabled people. Indeed, arguably, ending disablism would end the concept of disabled people, as the description would cease to have any meaning.

It would not end the natural disadvantages created by chronic ill health or pain. It would not alter the fundamental fact that being able to see, hear, walk, talk, chew, swallow, evacuate, ejaculate and control unwanted movements without assistance are all desirable skills. This does not mean that mobility by wheelchair is not efficient or acceptable, nor that there is any justification for placing artificial barriers such as steps in the way. However, given a free choice, most people would prefer the option of walking. This preference does not mean that those who cannot exercise the choice to walk are tragic, that their lives have less value, or that they should not share the same rights and responsibilities as other citizens.

The additional difficulties and discrimination which are created by people's reactions to disability are often worse than the impairment itself. These reactions range from pity to disgust and are equally unhelpful. The challenge for people who are interested in dismantling oppression is to seek a balance between the extreme positions of complete intolerance of disabled people on the one hand and total denial of the difficulties of impairment on the other.

This acceptance of the reality of the difficulties involved in having an impairment, and the recognition that life is made more difficult for disabled people by the discriminatory attitudes and actions of the majority, is only part of the picture. Life is not fair: some people are dealt better hands than others. Some are stronger, more gifted or more intelligent and few would deny the value of being born without impairment. That some are born with impairments is not entirely due to ill fate or bad luck. The deck from which the cards are being dealt is stacked: this is an unequal society in which some people and some communities experience greater degrees of poverty, ill health and lower educational standards. Neglect, ignorance, violence, drug abuse and poor health care all serve to create disability. Other children are born with impairments because of the inexactitude of medical science or as the result of medical error or experimentation. Society creates disabled children but fails to accept the responsibility for this by compensating the victims. Rather, it adds insult to injury by caring less for them than it does for children without impairments.

The last paragraph represents a way of understanding the position of disabled children, with which readers may agree or otherwise. What is perhaps more important to appreciate is that the vast majority do not understand or think about disabled children as an oppressed minority, and do not respond to them accordingly. If they do think about disabled children, and most people prefer not to, it is less likely to be as victims of an unequal and disabilist society than as unfortunate victims of fate. It is common to hear statistical probabilities of having a disabled child lobbed about so that people can assess the degree of risk involved. This is particularly common where there is more than one disabled child in the same family which can lead to a decrease in popular sympathy as the parents are seen as deliberately tempting an ill fate twice. In this way winning the lottery represents good fortune while a deformed child is bad luck. It is all in the stars. This effectively absolves society of any real sense of responsibility for the happiness or safety of the child. He or she should be grateful for what they are given.

Images are not always consistent and the situation of disabled children is confused for a number of reasons. Conan Doyle's story illustrates well the contradictory images of 'pathetic' and 'bad'. The reality is even more complex, since childhood is a transitory state.

Children are usually regarded as future adults and childhood is conceptualised as a preparation for adulthood. The expectations people have of growing children are age related, but reflect expectations of them as future adults. Children are taught skills and behaviours not only for the present, but to equip them for the adult life they are expected to lead. This learning is discriminatory, depending on what parents or society think is necessary and appropriate to teach and invariably has a gender bias.

The treatment of the child, in others words, shapes the adult they may become. This is an important concept for two reasons. First, it follows that to understand how we think of disabled children, we need some understanding of the world of the disabled adults they may become and for which we think we are preparing them.

Second, we need to explore the expectations we have of disabled children, and how we shape their childhood within society's understanding of the meaning of disability. There is a stark choice between educating children for a future state of dependency and non-contribution to society and educating them to be full and valued members. Disability is a learned state, and our upbringing of disabled children is a process of teaching inferiority: we teach disabled children that they are problems, of less value, and that they are not expected to fulfil the same gender roles as are non-disabled children. We ignore their childhood in our emphasis on making them function as *disabled*, rather than allowing them to enjoy themselves as children. Worse, when we prepare them for adulthood, it is for a disabled adulthood, which is seen as qualitatively of less value than an able-bodied one.

A disabled adult is viewed as less than a full citizen, as dependent: in fact, as occupying a permanent childlike status. The preparation of a disabled child for full adulthood is therefore overridden by their preparation for a life as a permanent child. As such, a disabled child is likely to experience neither a normal childhood, nor adolescence, and is conditioned into an adulthood of dependency. Whereas most children are envisaged as growing up to take the place of their parents, a disabled child is expected to remain a child. If the parents are abusers, a disabled child is not seen as one who will grow up to take revenge, and is therefore more vulnerable.

This is a vicious circle which can, and should be interrupted at every point, including directly challenging current attitudes towards disabled children: away from pathetic, burdensome and bad and toward children victimised because of their impairment, who have the right to a normal childhood.

In the long term, the success of the disability movement in improving things for disabled adults will improve the lives of disabled children as society starts to educate them to fit into a differing concept of life as a disabled adult.

Before enlarging on this theme, I want to take a look into the adult world, and work back from there into the world of the child. In doing that, I am very conscious that the world of disabled adults both in reality and in our imagery of it, is shaped not simply by adults who have grown up with disability but by adults who were raised as able-bodied children and became disabled in later life. This is a different journey than that taken by children who grow up with a disability. Adults who become disabled do not represent the adults that disabled children will become: they are, however, the most visible disabled adults, and they live with the same discrimination.

Images of disabled adults

In the Star Trek episode *'Ethics'*, the Klingon Worf is paralysed in an accident and, according to Klingon custom, asks for help in committing suicide. So central is the idea that life with a disability has no honour in it that the Klingons have a special ritual for assisted suicide, but devote no resources whatsoever to neurological research. The human view is emotionally presented by his friend Riker, who argues that paralysis does not mean that life is not worth living and that his friends and his young son would miss him. Worf is unmoved. (As a story dealing with the dilemmas of disability, it is then ruined by Worf subjecting himself to an experimental surgical procedure and becoming the first humanoid to have a successful spine transplant.)

In the real world, for Klingon, read 'male'.

There has been more analysis and more written about images of disabled adults than of children, possibly because adults are responsible for the writing. The most useful discussion is still probably that of Jenny Morris (1991). Readers interested in more academic analyses are also referred to the special edition of *Disability and Society*, Volume 9 number 3, published in 1994, devoted to representation and disabled people.

Although measuring and noting what appears on television screens does not necessarily tell us what remains fixed in people's cortexes, the findings of the Broadcasting Research Unit (1990) make interesting reading. They concluded that, if we believed our eyes watching television, we would know that there are not many disabled people in the world and that most of them are young and white. Able-bodied people are superior, while disabled people are pitiable and pathetic and/or bad. They are to be praised for perfectly normal acts, achieved despite their handicap, although some disabled people are exceptional 'supercrips'. Disabled people are likely to need medical help and are at high risk of dying during the programme or film.

While most images of disability may be created by an able-bodied culture as an attempt to distance itself from its fear, it is logical that such fears and feelings are internalised by people who become traumatically disabled, since they are not likely to wake up after a disabling incident with a new set of values. If there is no reappraisal, the result may be an inability to accept the change, with potentially devastating results. Many films and TV programmes, both factual and fictional, reinforce the view that becoming disabled is unbearably tragic, identify with the viewer's wish that the victim overcome their disability if possible, and their understanding should the disabled person choose death. The film *Whose Life Is It Anyway?* was a powerful reinforcer of the view that life without normal mobility is no life at all.

In the film *Born on the Fourth of July* based on the autobiography of Ron Kovic, two disabled Vietnam veterans express extreme distress at what is clearly meant to be a significant point in the story since it lasts so long, by circling each other in their wheelchairs shouting 'Fuck you!'... 'No, fuck you!' to each other. What seems on one level simply reinforcement of the paucity of language among American troops in Vietnam is, on another, a vicious and bitter expression of loss. The loss is of masculinity and with it any meaning in life. Veterans returning from Vietnam who had been disabled were very influential in the early disability movement, with the effect of flavouring it as a masculine protest movement in which some substitute for lost machismo had to be found. One result was an aggressive campaigning style characterised by marked hostility toward non-disabled people, rather than an attempt to educate or reach understanding. This hostility still marks much of the disability movement, reinforcing Conan Doyle's image of disabled people as jealous and consumed by hatred of those with whole or healthy bodies. It is an imagery which will readily appeal to unsympathetic able bodied people, much as the simplistic stereotyping of feminism as penis envy served misogyny.

A similar pattern of lost manhood and consequent self esteem can be identified on this side of the Atlantic. The real life case of PC Old will serve as illustrative. Old was a police motorcyclist before becoming disabled in the line of duty, and was made a hero by the press. He subsequently became idolised by many disabled youngsters as he defied medical science, refused to accept life in a wheelchair, and devoted himself to learning to walk using complex computer controlled electronic aides. It didn't work, and he committed suicide in October 1986. The tragedy in his story, and that of thousands of other men, was that the loss of ability to walk, and to have sex in the traditional manner, left him with no reason to be alive at all. The image of disability is about the loss of being a real man: swaggering, screwing, looking and feeling powerful and in control and playing football with a son. The perceived passivity and vulnerability of being in a wheelchair is hard to bear unless some rethinking is undertaken, or some substitute found. It seems easier where an intellectual career or outlet is possible, with the opportunity for intellectual thuggery, for those that need it, as a substitute for physical prowess. Similarly powerful positions can be found in organisations. It is worth noting, in passing, that the imagery we usually have of becoming disabled is almost exclusively around the trauma of sudden spinal injury, with confinement to a wheelchair as the consequence, rather than the much more common conditions such as arthritis or stroke.

For women, the situation is clearly different. Jenny Morris (1991) explores this theme in detail in *Pride against Prejudice*, and the disabled women who contributed to *Mustn't Grumble* also explore the dilemmas, pain and frustrations of being misunderstood and misrepresented by the dominant culture. (Keith 1994). Two ideas are important. First, that women are perceived as dependent in society anyway, so there is, clearly, less of a trauma for women who become disabled! Second, the loss of normality is seen as a loss of ability to be a standard woman: that is, heterosexual and a mother. Jenny Morris tells us she prefers to go shopping with her child because her presence gives her the illusory passport into the *'world of normal people. To assert that I am a mother is to distance myself from the abnormality of being disabled'* (Morris 1991, p36)

Society's current imagery of disabled adults is of people who lack normal gender roles, are dependent and vulnerable, but also stroppy, demanding and ungrateful. It is easier to accept polite and intellectual disabled people like Stephen Hawkins, although we are beginning to internalise the picture of the wise person with learning difficulties, who is simply on a different and less polluted wavelength. Nevertheless these are exceptional to everyday experience and will only affect our education of disabled children for those few who are seen as potentially exceptional themselves. For most, we continue to restrict learning opportunities and keep expectations low. We avoid explaining the risks of human relationships and keep the practicalities of sex a mystery, since disabled children are not expected to grow up to be fathers and mothers. We deny the chances offered to most children to learn by taking risks and to make choices that teach the skills of independence, since disabled adults are to be protected from risk and not expected to be independent. We ignore the fact of adolescence completely, as a life stage which does not apply to the genderless and asexual young disabled person.

In these ways our understanding of the world of disabled adults shapes our treatment of children, and assists prophecies to self fulfil as we pre-programme thousands of young people toward day centres, not employment.

The adult disability movement is seeking to change these understandings, with some success. However, many adult disabled people take the route of seeking not recognition of the rights of all disabled people, but inclusion into the able-bodied world by emphasising their own normality. This separates them from those disabled people who are 'less normal'. This is the effort to 'pass' which has accepted that able-bodied is best, or at least offers the better lifestyle, but which does not challenge discriminatory attitudes.

It is a pattern adopted by members of other oppressed groups from the light Indian who tried to pass for British in the days of the Empire, to the millions of gay people who pass as heterosexual. All these individuals contribute to the continued oppression of their own kind, although it is hard to deny the very real pressures they experience to behave in the way they do.

Both disabled women and men are pressured to emphasise their normality as mainstream men and women. This adds to the difficulties for those disabled people who cannot, or will not, try to fit. Disabled people from racial minorities, gays, and those with learning disabilities have to endure the additional marginalisation not only from mainstream, non-disabled society, but also from much of the disability movement, just as their disability marginalises them within their racial group, or from other gay people. Such forces also work against the development of alliances between these oppressed groups.

Images of disabled children

Disability is experienced as a loss of manhood, womanhood or motherhood for adults, but what does it mean for children? Exploring this issue as an adult carries the danger of becoming inextricably confused with what it means for parents. In trying to answer this question, we need to answer a number of others: what is perceived as normal childhood, and how are disabled children seen to differ from this? Is childhood disability so abnormal that such children are not perceived as children at all? What is society's image and expectation of a disabled child?

The following lists are taken from flip charts at a training day when a group of able bodied students were asked to brainstorm their ideas about images of disabled children. In my experience they are representative of the sort of comments that are typical at such events. Despite being asked to think about children, there is usually a noticeable tendency to think about the parents. They represent *images* held by non-disabled adults: the powerful majority.

Pity for mothers

Selfish to have a disabled child

Children are mistakes = blame/guilt/compensation

Guilt by children

Pain is worth it to become normal

Invisible

Exploited helping prisoners/old people

Not naughty

Vulnerable – need protection/care

Tragic Devoted parents Shielded from reality Gory details used by papers Strong/Determined Exploited by charity	Pity Different Inferior Reliant Can't work Costly
Die early Frail Isolated Cute when little Special resources	

The most common adjectives around disabled children are tragic and pitiable. Both these concepts apply equally, if not more strongly, to the parents. A common feature when asking groups to talk about disabled children is that, lacking any child-centred point of reference, they often identify with the adults in the family. 'Pity for the mother' often appears as, conversely, does 'selfish to have a disabled child'. 'Devotion' and 'charity' also crop up frequently. Parents shield their children from reality, feel guilty and seek to compensate. But what of the children themselves?

It is obvious from the struggle to find an imagery that, as far as the media goes, disabled children are largely invisible, except through presentation as children in need by various charities and through media fund-raising, usually on a local basis. So when people think of disabled children the imagery is of reliance on others, inferiority, costly and unlikely to work or do much to help themselves. They are envisaged as frail, isolated and likely to die early. When young they are cute, determined to overcome their disability, brave and grateful and thus encourage fund-raising. Anything achieved, however mundane, is against the odds, and such achievements are to be emphasised.

Like adults, disabled children are rare in films and television programmes and, if there at all, are likely to be portrayed as creating a tragic situation for their parents, or overcoming their disability. The film *Elephant Man* portrayed Merrick as a disappointment to his mother, who received a great deal of sympathy. Disability in that film was portrayed as a deviant, pathological state, in which Merrick was seen as not really even human. (Darke 1994) The film *My Left Foot* is based on the autobiography of Christie Brown, who had cerebral palsy, but which 'never moves beyond using disability as a metaphor for dependency' (Morris 1991 p95). The book is marketed as the story of a supercripple. According to the jacket of the Penguin version, Christie Brown is a 'giant of Irish literature', but the real selling point is the fascination that someone who could only use their left foot could write anything at all. (Brown 1954/1989) Disabled people are judged by different standards.

It is probably true to say that images of disabled children are more likely to be formed from documentaries and from charity advertising than from films and television fiction. These vary in the sort of image portrayed: the quality of reporting varies enormously depending on whether the presentation is designed to inform, sensationalise or extract money. Insidious messages can be transmitted when programmes ostensibly presented as informative documentaries make use of sensational techniques which confuse images in viewers' minds, and leave impressions which are inaccurate. In *Children's Hospital*, the story of Claire Howard who has achondroplasia and was receiving cosmetic treatment to make her taller, was juxtaposed with that of a child with life threatening liver disease. The confusion of disability with ill health was likely to stick in a viewer's mind, despite the fact that Claire had no pain and was in good health prior to her operation. The pain she underwent for several years to make her taller, the risk of infection, the immobility and the permanent scarring were thought necessary by her and her mother to counteract not a medical problem but to help her deal with the prejudice she would face because of her shortness of height. This programme reinforced the image of a courageous disabled child, undergoing major surgery in order to be more like the rest of humanity. She was performing as the dominant culture demands.

A rare exception to this portrayal of childhood disability as tragedy to be bravely overcome is the American film *When You Remember Me* which depicts a disabled child fighting the discrimination and bad practice he encounters in the residential care system. It is based, loosely, on the true story of Michael Patrick Smith, who had Duchenne Muscular Dystrophy. While there is much one might be picky about in the depiction of Michael by an able-bodied actor as rather too good to be true, the film is not about the horrors of disability, but about the way disabled children are ill treated. As such, it has features in common with the more famous *One Flew Over the Cuckoo's Nest* which challenged assumptions about mental ill health. There is even a nurse Ratchett look-alike. The film highlights issues of abuse by enforced medication, not being allowed to take risks such as attending a Grateful Dead concert and not being believed. It deals with the vulnerability of disabled children in a world designed by and run for the convenience of able-bodied adults and it is possible to forgive its occasional sentimentality in tackling these issues which are normally hidden from sight. William Horwood addresses similar themes in his book *Skallagrig*, which was subsequently made into a film of the same name.

Images of childhood

Another approach to understanding the world of disabled children is to explore how it differs from our understanding of the lives of non-disabled children.

Stereotypically, what is our understanding of normal childhood, and why is it that some children do not fit this? The birth of a child is usually cause for celebration and its parents are to be congratulated. A child is normally expected to reward its parents by looking like them, smiling, being cuddly, learning from its parents and others, and achieving at school. A child can cry, make mistakes, be naughty, be punished. The child is expected to be childish at the appropriate age but to grow up and out of dependency, eventually to form relationships outside the family, leave home and become independent and finally to care for the parents in their old age.

There are of course gender differences which must be learned. A baby has no idea what gender it is, but boys and girls are conditioned from a very early age into gender specific roles.

Adults behave differently toward boy babies and girl babies. Researchers have noted that adults respond differently to the perceived sex of a baby, bouncing boys and cuddling girls, on the simple stimulus of whether they are dressed in blue or pink (QED, 'He Man, She Man', BBC Television, 28.3.95). Boys and girls have different toys. Boys grow up learning to dominate, take up space and to dampen down their emotions, and 'real men' continue to practice these characteristics throughout adulthood. Girls learn to nurture, to defer, and not to interrupt. They learn the expectation that they will find a male partner and raise children, balancing career and motherhood if necessary. Both sexes learn that gender is polarised and that it is more difficult to negotiate life with feelings or behaviours that are ambiguous in gender terms.

Society constrains us to conform to gender stereotyped roles and, by and large, misfits are ill treated. As we grow older we learn new parts, often playing them in ways which relate to earlier learned gender behaviour. We may struggle with our identity, and perhaps rebel against the rigidity of its gendered expectations, in the end hopefully arriving at some understanding of who we are and what the point of it all is.

The journey for a disabled child is different, and differently understood. Much of this stereotyping is reversed. The birth is a tragedy, the parents to be commiserated with. The child will not reward its parents, learn anything or achieve at school. Disabled children are not naughty and should not be punished. They do not cry, but display great courage in the face of adversity. They do not grow up and out of their dependency, will never have sexual relationships nor care for others. There is not much difference in all this between disabled boys or girls. As such, like disabled adults, the presence of disability overrides gender identity.

Significantly, we very rarely hear of disabled boys or disabled girls. The phrase is nearly always the gender neutral 'disabled children'. Significantly also, there are toys for boys, toys for girls and toys for disabled children. In adulthood, the two genders and the genderless are represented by toilets: Ladies, Gents and Disabled. Disabled children are treated by adults not according to their gender, but according to their diagnosis. Just as a non-disabled baby has no idea of its gender until it is taught, a disabled child has no idea that it is disabled. It has to learn to behave as a *disabled* child because of adult behaviour towards it and expectations placed upon it. As with much of the adult response to non-disabled children, adults unconsciously transmit their own conditioned understanding of disability, which overrides the imprinted ideas of 'boy' or 'girl' or even of 'child'. Like their non-disabled peers, disabled children will grow up surrounded by this conditioning. Similarly disabled children have the ability to question their role, to rebel, to seek to be seen differently. Unlike them, there is less likely to be an adult role model to follow.

An optimistic conclusion from all this might be that a disabled child is free to avoid the sexual stereotyping forced on non-disabled children. The difficulty with this argument is that disability is seen not as a freeing condition, but a constraint, in which neither stereotypical male or female adult roles are perceived for the future, but one of asexuality, dependency and cost to the community.

The whole picture is one where disability as a negative forms the main theme, and the fact of childhood is lost. In stating this, I would not wish to suggest that the answer is to ignore the fact of disability, which is quite clearly part of the child's reality, but to recognise that it derives not simply from an impairment but from the complex reactions to it. I want to suggest that as a society we are still in danger of forgetting that disabled children not only have an essential humanity, but are also children, and that neither is currently respected in our day-to-day behaviour toward disabled children, despite its recognition in The United Nations Convention on the rights of the child, and its being enshrined in the law of the land. This says much about the relative lack of influence of the UN and Parliament compared with the more powerful folklore.

There is a great deal that parents and other adults can do to counter these patterns by emphasising the fact of childhood first, rather than the disability, and by responding to the child's personality rather than their diagnosis. In doing this the child is enabled to become central to the picture, and their experience of prime importance and value, displacing the medical practitioner as the source of expertise.

The experience of a disabled child is likely to be one of difference from others around her, and of generally negative reactions to that difference. The sense of aloneness or even the invisibility of her kind may be very strong. This is reinforced, particularly for girls, by the dearth of disabled children on television and in books and the very strong possibility that if a disabled child does appear, he will be cured by the end of the story, largely through his own good behaviour. The message is not only that disability is a bad thing, but that by trying hard enough it can be cured: this is not the reality for most disabled children. Such beliefs that effort and faith can cure disability persist even in adult minds, and encourage undue focus on futile and often costly remedial programmes which line the pockets of the providers who risk nothing in the process.

The place of disabled children in society is marginal. In seeking to address underrepresentation of minority groups in the media, activists have pointed out that diversity is part of human experience and should be celebrated as such. Disability is a fact of life and in hiding it fear and ignorance are made the more likely. The difficulty is that many people do not want disability to be a part of human experience, and not only seek to eliminate it from the media, but also from the real world. The message that disabled children receive about their lack of value in some eyes is not simply paranoia, it is very real. The problem is that the methods used in elimination of disability, both in the past in Nazi Germany and in the present throughout the world, involve the elimination of the whole child. This may be more sophisticated in the West than for the children who are left to die in Chinese orphanages, but it amounts to the same thing. Until we learn to put an equal value on the life of all children, we shall continue to disgrace ourselves as a society.

Part Two

Making A Difference

Chapter 4
Child Protection: A Key to Change

Introduction

Child protection work is the area of social work which attracts most attention, both within the profession and in the media. As such investing time and effort in it is essential to changing practice. This applies equally to changing practice for disabled children. The current system is deeply discriminatory at all levels and any attempts to change things must recognise this. Disabled children are currently largely invisible in mainstream child protection: on caseloads in child protection teams, on child protection registers, in case conferences, in the courts, in research and in literature.

By focusing on how disabled children are to be protected, we have to address issues such as their fundamental right not to be abused; issues of equality of opportunity with non-disabled children; the rights and responsibilities of parents; the operation of the judicial system and the organisation of services.

In trying to make a positive difference for disabled children child protection is neither a separate issue nor an alternative to working with them. It should not be avoided by 'disability' specialists as outside their concern, since improving child protection is fundamental to demonstrating concern for the value of disabled children and a key to better practice. There is a clear need for their skills and knowledge in extending the capacity of child protection services to include children who are different.

It is simply not enough to state that policy and procedures apply to all children. Disabled children frequently receive a different quality of response than that offered to non-disabled children despite the overwhelming evidence that disabled children are victims of abuse. Such evidence is neither new nor in dispute (see Westcott and Cross 1995 for a comprehensive research bibliography). There have been few corresponding improvements in service delivery. In child protection perhaps more than in any other area of social work it has been possible to ignore the existence of disabled children, as if they were not really children at all and neither needed nor deserved protection. This failure to protect is reinforced and condoned by a judicial system from which disabled children are effectively excluded.

There are indications that this is changing. I have encountered considerable genuine embarrassment from social workers, team managers and social work educators about the paucity of service offered to disabled children, but the embarrassment stems from perceived ignorance of an unfamiliar group, rather than from an awareness of institutionalised discriminatory practices. They therefore regard the 'solution' to be to increase their knowledge about medical conditions, not to find ways of extending good child-care practice. It is as inappropriate to draw conclusions from diagnosis, as it would be to stereotype according to racial background. It is not ignorance of disability that is the problem but fear of difference.

Much that is written about child protection assumes it is the parents, or someone else within the home who commit the abuse. Abuse perpetrated outside of families is very much a reality for many disabled children and social services should have clear policies on dealing with this. Parents have to be alert and to be prepared to insist on the same rigour of investigation and level of action against the perpetrator as they would expect if the child were non-disabled. The principle is the same as should be adopted with any other service provider, which is to avoid placing the blame on the child because they are different from most children, and to insist that the authorities take action which acknowledges the particular characteristics of the child. This may involve the use of an interpreter, for example.

For all the above reasons I considered that child protection merited special attention in a separate chapter, but the decision to deal with it in this way was not an easy one. I am conscious that doing so may imply that child protection is something distinct from other childcare practice. This is not my intention. Nor do I subscribe to the view that it requires a different sort of worker or range of skills from childcare in general, although there is clearly a distinctive knowledge base. This chapter will also argue strongly that disabled children receive a poorer quality service by reason of their disability. Readers should not take that to mean that as a whole child protection services do not need improvement. This is clearly not the case. Indeed, I believe that in reviewing child protection services with a view to protecting disabled children adequately, it will be possible for service providers to offer suggestions for improvement for children as a whole.

The chapter starts by exploring the discrimination faced by disabled children and by emphasising their right to be included in protection services, and then reviews some of the overarching issues around child protection in general. It then moves on to consider the practice issues involved in developing services for disabled children. In this, I have tried to move the debate on from the dawning realisation that 'something must be done' to begin to explore what this may mean for social workers.

Policy issues

Legally, a disabled child has as much right to protection as any other. The local authority has the duty under the Children Act to investigate where there is 'reasonable cause to suspect that a child who lives, or is found, in their area is suffering, or is likely to suffer, significant harm' (Section 47 (1) (b) and to consult with other agencies if necessary to take steps to protect the child. The authority has a duty to safeguard and protect the welfare of the child, and bring proceedings to facilitate the investigation if information is refused. There are resource implications here and it is usual for investigative work to claim resources as a priority. This has been strongly challenged as an inefficient use of social work time, which could have been more effectively directed toward facilitating access to services (Rose 1995).

This situation is particularly difficult for disabled children where any emphasis on collecting evidence towards prosecution as a priority is likely to deny them any protection at all, as disabled children are seen as less credible as informants. In addition, abuse or neglect is assumed to be hard to distinguish from the physical, developmental or emotional abnormalities associated with or attributed to their impairment. This is compounded by the complementary prejudices that disabled children have less value than non-disabled children and that since parents of disabled children are under more pressure than most parents, abuse is therefore often thought to be more excusable.

The failure to offer the same degree of protection is discriminatory. It is rooted and reflected in social services structures which often marginalise or even ignore the protection of disabled children. There remain deep-seated, and deeply mistaken, beliefs that disabled children are not subjected to abuse. These combine with a paralysis of will created by service providers who simply do not know what to do. The usual responses, the appropriateness of which could be debated, such as removing at risk children to foster carers seem unavailable where children have high care needs.

The protection needs of disabled children were conspicuously absent from the large amount of research commissioned by the Department of Health after Cleveland, summarised in the document *Child Protection: Messages from research*, although there is one passing reference to disabled children as 'special victims' which relates to the 'special problems facing some parents' (DOH 1995: p 21). This neglect reflects the capacity at all levels to separate thinking about disability from issues around protection. *Messages from research* conceptualises child abuse as socially constructed, reflecting the values of a society. If this is essentially true, it follows that the official failure to deal with the abuse of disabled children reflects a cultural lack of concern for their welfare. Disabled children will only be better protected when we learn as a society to value them equally.

Failure to have abuse on the agenda at all has a number of causes.

People are not sensitised to the possibility of abuse in the same way that they are with non-disabled children. Behaviours which in a non-disabled child might be interpreted as indicating unhappiness are ascribed to the disability (i.e. part of the normal characteristic of a disabled child's behaviour pattern). Challenging behaviour is almost always blamed on the disability. Children who behave in an overtly sexual manner should alert adults to the possibility of abuse, but this possibility is less often on the agenda of those who care for disabled children. Social workers, healthcare professionals and educationalists need to be aware.

There is a genuine issue about lack of confidence among disability specialists in dealing with child protection, which is fed by the often macho approach exuded by child protection work. These issues must be tackled by the organisation in terms of inclusion in training and of updating on procedures. A social worker who can communicate well with a disabled child will make a good child protection worker, given the right support and backing. More genuine fears about competence ought to be raised when social workers refuse to work with disabled children because of their own perceived inability to communicate with them. These areas of lack of confidence mean that many of the arguments around the appropriate siting of child protection services are made on false premises. At the end of the day many are based on an underlying assumption that the protection of disabled children is a separate and lower priority task. Some social services departments are still side lining child protection where the child is disabled.

Given the existence of the Children Act and the publicity from the NSPCC, it is no longer possible to believe that the message has not been heard that disabled children are vulnerable to abuse. Failure to provide the same level of protection as for non-disabled children has to be interpreted neither as a sin of omission nor as ignorance, but as a deliberate policy that needs challenging. Westcott and Cross (1995) argue that, as disabled people are an oppressed group, it follows that perpetrators have a 'licence' to abuse. The implications of this are that organisations can choose not to protect, or can neglect this duty with impunity.

This is not to imply that non-disabled children receive a good service. Indeed, a change in the direction of childcare and the prevention of abuse would benefit all vulnerable children. It may very well be that social services departments are paralysed not so much by a lack of awareness that the problem exists but a lack of ideas at a professional level about what can be done, and a lack of commitment at either a political or a managerial level to find out.

While I cannot agree with such inaction, I have some sympathy with those who chose other avenues for their energy, for a number of reasons. Advocating for disabled children may be a minority interest, but it is fraught with all the pitfalls around political correctness which have troubled much more popular causes such as anti-racism and the protection of women from domestic violence. Much that is written on the subject by researchers, including disabled people, describes the shortcomings of the current situation but risks few suggestions about practical ways forward. Despite the efforts of some individuals, there is no sense of widespread outrage or demands to protect disabled children either from pressure groups or from the voting public as a whole. Indeed parents or others who care for disabled children are more likely to be regarded by the public as saints. Local politicians are acutely aware of their public, which disempowers professionals who wish to make any changes that might be perceived as stealing resources from popular causes.

The world of child protection services

In seeking to explore what kind of protection services are to be recommended, it is worth remembering that we are not trying to set up services for disabled children from scratch. This would involve seeking to make appropriate connections between the growing understanding of their vulnerability and devising matching service responses: nothing so straightforward! We are entering a service area fraught with debate, under the cultural influence of the judicial system, driven by political priorities and subject to frequent trial by media.

The journalistic debate is simplistic and one track, operating around the question of: 'At what stage should social workers *act*?' (by which they mean remove the child from home) rather than 'What kind of support does this family need?' There is an enduring myth that removal from home into 'care' is an instant and easy solution to child abuse, and that all the social worker has to do is establish the innocence or guilt of the parents. Media judgement of the action or otherwise of the social worker as right or wrong depends on the perceived accuracy of this decision. Innocence or guilt is a distinction which is unhelpful in practice and adds fuel to the atmosphere of suspicion with which many people view social workers. This deters them from seeking or accepting help. In fuelling this atmosphere of blame, non-understanding and suspicion, journalism increases pressure on parents who are struggling, which in turn can only serve to increase the likelihood of children being abused.

Even the less shallow debates around child protection often seem more helpful to legal and political reputations than to professionals seeking ways forward in dealing with the complexities and dilemmas on the ground.

Worse still, these arguments take place within an adversarial culture predicated on the allocation of blame, rather than within any problem solving or co-operative framework. What drives someone to abuse a child seems of far less interest to lawyers and politicians than whose heads will roll as a result. The legal profession is trained and used to working in a gladiatorial arena which has winners and losers, guilty and innocent, and knows no shades in between. Lawyers have been entrusted with enquiry after enquiry after the death of a child from non-accidental injury, leaving us with increasingly refined mechanisms for allocating blame but no nearer to resolving the underlying problems either of what causes the abuse or the best way to protect children. As a result social workers in child protection learn to watch their backs and follow the rules. It has become a dangerous game; not least for the children who must trust themselves to the system.

If investigation with a view to a court hearing is started, it is necessary to understand the implications of that for disabled children and to acknowledge that the odds are heavily weighted in favour of the abuser.

Most child abuse cases do not come to court. Nevertheless the courts and the lawyers who service them are incredibly influential in setting the adversarial tone which characterises child protection services as a whole, and it is worth spending a little time in understanding this. Social services departments might like to consider exactly why their services are organised in the way they are and how much their systems are driven by approaches to child protection derived from the victim/perpetrator/punishment culture of the judicial system. It can be argued that not only do the courts fail individual children in making it impractical to seek redress there, but they also represent the failure of the judicial system as a whole to protect them.

The police are part of this process and the attitude of the police officers involved with both children and suspected abusers may be crucial. The collection and recording of evidence of abuse can be more difficult where the child is disabled. Disabled children may be even less likely to tell a worker directly, especially if there are communication difficulties, and it is therefore necessary to ask! The police officer has been exposed like any other adult to discriminatory attitudes and messages about disabled children, and is just as likely as anyone else to feel embarrassed at communication difficulties, be less willing to believe what is being said and to experience distress at having to deal with an abused child. The police will be involved in investigations into sexual abuse and need to reach some understanding with social workers about the aims of the investigation and both possible and desirable outcomes. Issues about disabled children need to be built into the joint training now undertaken by police and social workers.

People such as paediatricians and police surgeons also require training to think of disabled children as possible victims and it is important to ensure that children are examined by medical practitioners who have some understanding in this area. Defining significant harm can be more complicated where there is chronic ill health or developmental delay, but it would be quite wrong not to question the care a child is receiving. This is probably even more important where the child is living away from home.

There are major stumbling blocks to integrating child protection work when punishing the offender becomes more important than protecting the child. The requirements of the criminal courts for credible witnesses work against victims of abuse, and create a vicious circle where the police, the Crown Prosecution

Service and social workers lose interest in pursuing cases of abuse unless a successful prosecution seems likely.

Instances of disabled children, or adults, giving evidence in court are rare. As a rule, disabled children are seen as less able to give evidence in court, or less likely to be believed when they do.

The courts are very much at fault here, and need to change fundamentally not only to enable children to give evidence, but to accept it on a different basis than at present. Moves to help children give evidence without exposure to cross-questioning in open court by use of video links have proved unpopular with prosecutors because they know that a child in genuine distress in the courtroom will carry more weight with judge or jury. This is a shameful indictment.

The current adversarial system, which seems to be geared more to imitating television than finding the truth, relies too much on drama to convince judges and juries. The system puts the burden of proof on the witness and is heavily weighted against them. A court is a white, male, able-bodied, adult-orientated arena, in which women and children victims are ill served. The vicious circle of non-prosecution means most perpetrators of crimes such as domestic assault, rape and sexual abuse get away with it, sending an obvious message both to abusers and victims.

Social workers need to be realistic about this when working with children. In seeking to get children to talk some workers have been guilty of making false promises. Letting a child believe that the perpetrator will be 'put away' is dishonest and can generate a deep sense of betrayal for the child (Sharland et al 1995).

These difficulties should strengthen the case for a confident organisational response from social services departments to challenge the way the courts operate. More fundamentally social services departments should examine the whole ethos of their childcare practice. Action to support and protect children should not be dependent on the perceived chances of the perpetrator being punished.

This may seem complicated in a world where auditors demand hard evidence of activity. Children's names placed on the Child Protection Register or cases taken to court are more easily measured than children who were protected from harm by the provision of counselling or additional help at home. Departments seeking change should be encouraged to make use of the message from the

Audit Commission published in 1994, which indicated that billions of pounds of social services' budgets for childcare were being misdirected every year. The enormous amount of research commissioned in recent years by the Department of Health seems broadly to agree on the need to move away from the collection of evidence for At Risk Registers toward improving service access. (DOH 1995). While these research findings can be used to push for resources, they should be viewed with some caution. I doubt many child protection workers really viewed placing a child on a register as an end in itself so much as a pragmatic recognition that having the child's name on the list may be the only means of securing scarce resources.

Auditors too need to learn to think differently.

The academic or theoretical debate can be equally unhelpful. There are longstanding and diversionary false dichotomies which plague debates about child protection and hinder the development of services. They add grist to both legal and academic mills but many are essentially artificial and create spurious conflicts.

One is the notion of the pendulum which swings between the rights of the child and that of the parent, according to the latest child abuse scandal. The rights of the child were strengthened after the Maria Colwell inquiry. Parental rights were loudly invoked after Cleveland. This polarisation is not necessary within a model of practice which places the *interests* of the child centrally, and expects parents to accept that they have *responsibilities* toward them. This unhelpful debate sets investigation and rescue, with a view to prosecution if possible, as alternatives to support for families, which creates space for unnecessary debates about their relative importance or value. Much of it is reflected in the language and attitudinal sets of organisations and workers. 'Investigation', 'case', 'assessment'and 'register' are loaded words, and create fear and defensiveness. 'Finding out', 'talking about' and 'taking notes' might be more helpful concepts. If it proves necessary, 'investigation' will be easier and more accurate where support and understanding are offered. Most parents do not wish to abuse their children, nor allow others to do so. This is the essential dynamic with which most child protection services should work.

The enduring and sterile arguments about the relative responsibility of parents and social workers occur in an atmosphere where there is little balancing political, legal or journalistic effort to sponsor positive change or to ease the tensions which set parents and those who should be helping them against each other. As such the concept of partnership in the Children Act is developing a hollow ring. Social workers are expected to search out and identify problem parents, while parents are conditioned to defend themselves from professional interference. This does not just apply to social work: I was struck by a comment from a mother at a recent conference who confessed to responding instinctively to routine enquiries from the health visitor about her children's progress with automatic reassuring nods that all was well, whatever the truth of the matter. How much more likely are parents who are experiencing real difficulties to lie to an official widely stereotyped as one who takes children away from home?

If it starts from a supportive rather than a punitive perspective, good practice allows parents safely to express their own anxieties about possible abuse within the family. The concept of child protection as a 'rescue' service is prevalent and intimidating. A culture which typecasts all abusers as villains, is unlikely to encourage parents under stress to approach it for help. This applies equally to a parent who is driven to hit a child as it does to a mother who knows her partner is sexually abusing her child. Fear will also prevent the parent who neglects her disabled child by leaving her in bed or locking her alone in the house from seeking help. A rescue orientated service relies on having somewhere to rescue the victim to. The absence of appropriate foster or residential care for disabled children means that no service at all is offered to protect. This is depressing head-in-the-sand thinking in that child protection workers are paralysed into inaction because the standard solution is unavailable. Rather than doing nothing, the options seem to be either to develop residential and foster care services for disabled children or to think of a better way forward: such as offering support in the home.

Organisations can work in partnership with parents in the interests of child protection given an approach from the professional which understands the range of abuse to which a child is vulnerable both outside the family and within it.

Partnership is being actively promoted by the Department of Health as a reasonable approach to working with parents during child abuse cases. The research message is that with the exception of some extreme cases where parents are antagonistic or the abuse very serious, the quality and extent of partnership between parent and professional are major factors influencing the outcome of the case (DOH 1995). Despite this, it acknowledges that partnership was not achieved in many cases, for which it blamed agency policies and social work practice.

If partnership is to become a reality there is need for change not only in social work practice, but also in the political and social climate in which it has to operate. This may be one of those chicken-and-egg situations where social workers may have to try to make partnership work despite the odds. However partnership is not a rosy alternative to professional/client. It contains a built in contradiction since its status as a voluntary working relationship can be enforced by law if necessary and one of the partners is always going to be more powerful than the other.

Social workers need to be aware of the pitfalls of adopting the slogan without working through what it means for all parties and should appreciate the difficulties involved in getting alongside troubled and vulnerable people. Parents are not always rational and sensible, any more than social workers are always patient and understanding. Nevertheless, if the starting-point is a belief that most children are better off within their own family, parenting needs to be adequate rather than perfect, since the options are almost invariably worse. Parents need to be helped to be 'good enough'. Given this baseline, there are only a small number who should never be allowed to parent.

This is not to deny the difficulty for social workers in achieving a supportive role, particularly in the current anti welfare culture, but to emphasise the appropriateness of such an approach. Support means dealing with underlying problems on a broad basis, not simply acting as an ambulance service when things go wrong. This means improvements in education, housing and leisure facilities, and tackling issues like poverty and racism. In professional care, it means putting the interests of the child first and being prepared to tackle poor institutional practices. The continuing existence of multi-disciplinary and inter-agency working in child protection is a hopeful sign and a potential source of strength.

Abuse of disabled children

As one chapter in a short book covering a range of service issues for disabled children, this section is not intended to cover everything about child abuse, but to set in it a context of service development. Readers are recommended to read the Venture Press book by Helen Westcott and Merry Cross (1995) and the NSPCC Training Resource Pack (1993) for practice guidance, as well as making critical use of standard texts on child protection. Even though many of the latter make scant reference to disability, it makes no sense to reinvent the wheel where there are developed wisdoms about prevention, protection and working with survivors. The relative absence of work with, and literature about, disabled children who are abused means that, in turn, good practice is failing to be fed into the system. An understanding of the causes of abuse would be helpful in working out preventive strategies. The difficulties with this are twofold. First, although there are many commonalties, each case is different. Second, despite a wealth of research both the causes of abuse and the best ways to prevent it are still contested areas.

Following the Cleveland enquiry in 1989 the Department of Health recognised the dearth of research into effective practice in child protection and funded a substantial number of studies, none of which focused on issues for disabled children. Nor were any of the studies designed to discover the causes of abuse, from which I can only assume that the Department of Health did not wish to know!

The results of twenty of these studies are summarised in *Child Protection: Messages from Research* (DoH 1995) which the Department call important messages for policy and practice. In terms of protecting children, there are five conditions identified as significant in effective practice to protect children:

1 sensitive and informed professional /client relationship;

2 an appropriate balance of power between participants;

3 a wide perspective on child protection;

4 effective supervision and training of social workers;

5 services which enhance children's general quality of life.

The DOH admits that moving from a famine to a feast of research findings may have confused rather than clarified the situation. At both first and second glance the findings appear to contain nothing new, nor anything anyone could argue with. No one would seriously suggest that the professional client relationship should be insensitive or ill informed. Unfortunately it does not take us any further forward in practical terms, except perhaps to strengthen the case for practitioners in arguing for better supervision and better quality childcare services as a basis from which to operate.

This continuing lack of consensus about the detail of what helps and what hurts does not assist the practitioner in seeking guidance to find the best way to protect vulnerable children. There is a real need for more practitioner-based research in this field. It may turn out that what really helps most are well-educated practitioners who are able to think for themselves, but I am conscious that in the current climate of NVQs this is a highly controversial suggestion. Educators may take comfort from the Department of Health's own recommendation that

> *because professionals involved in child protection are influential, it is clear that their competence is more than a matter of simply adhering to the rules and following guidance; they need to display sensitivity and discretion combined with forceful curiosity*
>
> (DOH 1995, page 48)

While we wait for some better understanding, I have adopted a pragmatic approach to the issue based on what we know already: disabled children are more vulnerable and suffer abuse and existing services are discriminatory. We need to look for ways to correct the balance in favour of services which are in the child's interests. I have taken the view that this will normally also be the wish of the parents. Nevertheless it needs to be acknowledged that there are pressures on families which can lead them to abuse and to collude with abuse, particularly that which happens in health, education and welfare provision. It is important for social workers to find ways to help parents to act in their child's best interests. These are not issues that will be resolved on an individual basis, but require collective action, as well as a backdrop of training for parents and professionals, shared care and social workers, doctors and teachers with time to listen. As such a community work model may be more helpful than a casework or counselling approach.

As a general caveat, I suspect I have not always differentiated between the different sorts of abuse at each and every opportunity. Abuse can be neglect, physical, racial, institutional, emotional and/or sexual and all apply to disabled children. Much of my own thinking about abuse of disabled children has been informed from the perspective of sexual abuse, and what follows may reflect this bias and utilise its language. The concepts of perpetrators and victims (or survivors) are from the world of sexual abuse. Survivors of sexual abuse have become more visible and vocal and influenced thinking in a way which survivors of physical abuse have not. There is a distinct difference in the minds of most people between the outrage felt about the sexual abuse of children and the understanding offered to frustrated parents who hit out at or shake their children. The police are much more likely to be involved in the investigation alongside the social worker if the allegations are of child sexual abuse: indeed such joint working is required in such cases (Home Office 1991)

As a society we are more understanding of the physical abuse of children since it is perceived as the action of normal people provoked by stress, unlike sexual abuse which is the activity of 'perverts' and which is known to result in long-term psychological problems for the child. I am grateful to Stella Coleman for reminding me that despite this qualitative difference, it is physical abuse which is more likely to result in the death of the child, whether by acts such as shaking or by more deliberate acts of cruelty.

Social workers in contact with disabled children all need an awareness of the issues around physical and sexual abuse; some strategies for reducing risk; a commitment to equality for disabled children and to taking appropriate action on their behalf.

First, it may be necessary to ditch some myths.

- Disabled children *are* abused, and vulnerable to a wider range of abuse from a greater number of possible sources than non-disabled children. Their disability renders them more vulnerable, and perpetrators of sexual abuse seek out vulnerable victims. This does not mean it is the child's fault.

- Disabled children experience the same range of abuse as any children: neglect, physical harm, sexual and emotional abuse. They are easier to hurt because of their impairment. A child who needs callipers also needs them to fit properly and to be put gently on her legs. A child who cannot feed herself needs whoever wields the spoon to do so carefully. Westcott and Cross have a disturbing range of examples for those who need convincing or enlightening (Westcott and Cross 1995). I will mention just one: my own first encounter with an abused disabled child (as far as I know). This concerned a teenager who was simply left at home all day while her mother was at work. She was unable to do anything to help herself, and by evening she was cold, hungry, incontinent and in pain. Social workers need to open their minds to the possibilities of abuse or neglect that exist by virtue of the disability.

- Parents who injure disabled children out of frustration are more readily understood than those who injure non-disabled children because of the stereotyped belief that disabled children are more difficult to raise. This does not make the abuse any more acceptable.
- A disabled child experiences the trauma of abuse just as any other child does. It matters just as much, both at the time and afterwards.
- Disabled children are no more nor less likely to tell lies than any other children.
- Far from being a safe haven, residential care is a high-risk environment where disabled children can be isolated and without advocates. This has been repeatedly demonstrated from Maureen Oswin (1984) to Jenny Morris (1995). Residential staff do not always demonstrate respect for residents which can create a culture in which abuse is less likely to be condemned, and therefore becomes more likely to occur.

Research such as that cited above reminds us forcibly of the nature and extent of abuse, and urges vigilance and outrage. I am concerned to ensure that such outrage leads social workers and others to look for practical steps to improve the situation. I must also emphasise that such improvement should be part and parcel of regenerating childcare services in general, not a specialist and different service created to deal with a specific problem. I prefer to approach the issue of abuse as part of the key theme of developing anti-oppressive practice on behalf of the child, and of working with parents. This is for two reasons:

First, it is to illustrate and emphasise that child protection is not a form of social work that can be neatly split off from other work with families. In practice, this often happens for organisational reasons. Child protection and childcare for disabled children may be organisationally separated from each other and/or from services for non-disabled children. Despite the existence of these organisational splits, I see no sound professional reasons for promoting them. As well as encouraging an elitist, macho approach to child protection as something more important that other childcare work, it also promotes the idea that parents who abuse are somehow different from parents in general, rather than people caught up in situations they cannot handle, which leads me to the second issue.

An anti-oppressive approach would seek to avoid the danger of polarisation between the interests of the child and that of the parents. While I am anxious to argue that their needs are different, and may well be in conflict on occasion, the notion of a bad parent in one corner and a child and the social worker in another is equally unhelpful. It cannot be denied that there are some callous and deliberately cruel individuals in this world, who should not be allowed anywhere near children. However, I think it is important to start from the premise that while they may experience enormous frustration and anger with their child's behaviour most parents consider hurting children to be wrong and can exercise restraint most of the time.

Child protection services have been guilty of organising all services around the worst-case scenario, rather than being more widely directed also to support parents on the understanding that experiencing the urge to hit out at children is quite common: indeed the research evidence indicates that most parents hit their children, even those under the age of one (DOH 1995). This does not make it right although such action is described by the Department of Health as 'normal behaviour within families' and much physical abuse therefore construed as discipline gone wrong (DOH 1995:p12). This conceptualisation of hitting children as 'normal' because it is common practice is counter productive since its 'normality' avoids taking responsibility as a society to think about better ways to raise children. Being widespread does not necessarily render a practice acceptable. In this case, it should mean there are opportunities for tackling the issue of child abuse by finding ways to improve childcare standards in general.

There is less help available than there might be in helping parents to understand why their children may behave badly, nor is there adequate support for many parents in sharing the care. Children who seek attention or help have a range of options at their disposal, and this dynamic is no different for a disabled child, although the actual behaviours utilised may be dictated by their impairment. Children who cannot slam out of a room may more readily resort to screaming, biting or refusing to eat. Society oppresses such children by not offering them support through their parents and then adds injury to insult by overlooking it if they are physically abused as a result. A measure of abuse is tolerated and understood because of the difficult or challenging behaviour. Margaret Flynn translated this for me as 'eloquent' behaviour: a more accurate description since the child is clearly trying to communicate something. Parents can thus get caught up in an oppressive, disabilist system and become the instruments of abuse of their own children.

Finally, both common sense and research findings indicate that the outcome is more satisfactory where parents are involved in the protection process (DOH 1995).

Dealing with abuse

1. Reducing Risk
It is always better to prevent harm than try to pick up the pieces later. There are a number of things that both organisations and social workers can be doing in order to reduce risk.

First, while strategies to help children protect themselves are being developed, largely in relation to sexual abuse from strangers, it is important to remember that the responsibility for protection lies clearly with adults. There is a danger, if self-help fails, that the child will suffer a double insult of being abused and of feeling it is their own fault. It is also highly likely that disabled children will fail to relate safety programmes to themselves, since the children portrayed are normally able-bodied. Helen Westcott and Merry Cross have a long discussion about the merits and dangers of protection programmes (Westcott and Cross 1995).

Disabled children are in danger of blaming themselves for being sexually abused, given high risks of low self-esteem and a belief that their disability is a bad thing. Victim blaming is common in many forms of crime. Rape is a very obvious example. Self-blame is prevalent with abused children, and it is vital for the social worker to try to convince the child that abuse of any kind is not, and can never be, their responsibility. It is important to remember that this is an issue for physical as well as for sexual abuse: disabled children are likely to blame themselves.

The combination of a belief that the abuse is their fault, of being a child, and of perhaps being told by the perpetrator to keep silent is a powerful disincentive to report abuse. It is essential that workers are sensitised to the possibilities of abuse, and prepared to act on what they are told or observe. These responsibilities are not simply, or even primarily, for social workers. Those in closer day-to-day contact with children such as teachers have a vital role to play. Workers in institutions have to be prepared to accept responsibility for standards within them and to encourage open debate about good and bad practice, predicated on the best interests of the child.

Children may feel ambivalent about the abuser. They may like him. It is perhaps an unpalatable fact, but many child abusers are liked by the children they abuse. This is a particular dilemma for many children who are sexually abused. Children can want the abuse to stop, without necessarily wanting the abuser to disappear. It is the behaviour that should be condemned, and most social workers will retain a belief in the possibility of human change for the better as a part of their philosophy. The sad fact is that many perpetrators of sexual abuse seem unlikely to respond to treatment or entreaty: they enjoy what they do (Howitt 1995).

In some families, and with less serious abuse, it may be possible to ensure that the child and abuser are not left alone together and that other members of the family take on responsibility for policing the situation. All the same, it does need to be acknowledged that separation is often the only appropriate preventive measure, and that it needs to be carefully handled. As with non-disabled children, it is the perpetrator who should be the one to go. Breaking up a family is no more or less bad news when the child is disabled, and yet there is a persistent differential weighting by some workers. In the same discriminatory way, Helen Westcott and Merry Cross (1995) report disabled survivors who recount investigations into possible abuse of their non-disabled siblings, which ignored the possibility that they might also have suffered.

If child abuse is an abuse of power, it follows logically that reducing the power of the perpetrator will reduce risk. It may not be that simple, however, since this tactic could merely divert his attention to someone even weaker. As a long-term strategy, it could well be that increasing people's sense of importance and raising their self-esteem would make more sense. In this context, addressing the sort of areas that disadvantage people would help: unemployment, poor housing, dead-end jobs, harassment at work, and so on. Bullying at work should be viewed as part of a possible chain of abuse which can end in the domestic sphere, affecting women and children.

In the pecking order, disabled children are the least powerful, and may attract abuse from others who feel powerless or bullied. The low rate of prosecutions of perpetrators of abuse makes this a fairly safe outlet.

While most parents do not wish to allow anyone to abuse their children, this may change under pressure. Parents can be part of the abusive system by not adequately challenging the bad practice or abuse of others. Philippa Russell points out that extreme pressure may force a parent to collude with bad practice, since the alternative is no help at all:

> *This mother suspected a worker at a residential home which she used for occasional respite of physically abusing her child. But she said, 'we parents become part of the collusion that it's all right. There are so few places for disabled children to go....We all have to play the game of maintaining the status quo. I can't blame the social workers. I do it too – but I don't sleep at night when she is away.'*
>
> (Russell 1994)

Abuse can be promulgated against disabled children in a wide variety of ways and settings, and it is worth the social worker taking time to explore with parents and with children their own fears about this. Much of it may be unthinking and tackled by either the parent or social worker talking with those responsible. The parents may know in which circumstances they feel their child is vulnerable, and it may be possible to explore with them how they can be made to feel safer. Parents may need to work together on this. One group successfully campaigned for a second helper on the school bus, because of fears of leaving children who could not communicate with any ease in the sole charge of one adult. This kind of action reduces risk without having to wait for the existence of abuse. As a policy, it not only helps parents' peace of mind, but also denies any potential abuser the opportunity of applying for the post of sole carer! Collective action is much more effective in such situations than a single parent going it alone, which invariably leads to their being labelled as awkward and the response that 'no one else has complained'.

This does not deal with everyone, even if it were an achievable end. There are some paedophiles who enjoy abusing children, and who will actively seek employment opportunities that facilitate this. It is important therefore to reduce their opportunities.

Westcott and Cross (1995) argue that contracts with providers should insist on rigorous vetting of staff, training for staff, a policy on abuse, procedures for reporting and a charter for children. Schools should be asked about their policies on intimate care.

Vetting is not an effective screening device and should not be allowed to lead to a sense of false security. Perpetrators do not have 'sexual abuser' stamped on their foreheads, and some vetting procedures concentrate their efforts by focusing on sexual behaviour and picking out categories of people thought to be perpetrators. Gay men have suffered a great deal of unjustified harassment because of unwarranted connections between homosexuality and child sexual abuse, despite the hard evidence being that most sexual abuse is committed by heterosexual males.

Police checking is clearly appropriate as one measure, but we know that perpetrators are rarely prosecuted, may not have a criminal record, and move from job to job. They are too often permitted to leave without disciplinary action. Organisations should be willing to listen when colleagues are prepared to 'whistle blow', and put the interests of children first. At the very least organisations have to be seen to be tough on sexual abusers so that perpetrators may be deterred from application.

These are organisational issues, but social workers have a role in influencing conditions where they work and, increasingly, in their role of care managers, in the organisations with which they contract for service. Children should not be exposed to high-risk situations, such as unaccompanied male supervision, hospital porters or taxi drivers.

Residential care is dangerous. The Utting review of residential childcare recognised this in its recommendation that the independent visitor scheme as set out in the Children Act (Schedule 2, para 17) be extended to include disabled children (Morris 1995). Removing children from family and community constitutes poor childcare practice, particularly for black children. Children in residential care are powerless and 'voiceless' (Westcott and Cross). Jenny Morris talks of 'institutional neglect' where there is a failure to promote emotional and educational well being (Morris 1995: p 62). If we follow a model of abuse as an abuse of power down the pecking order, we know that residential staff are low paid, low status workers. This felt powerlessness, together with the permission of a disabilist society to abuse disabled children, puts children in care at great risk. It follows that keeping children out of residential care, including residential schooling, will reduce risk of abuse.

Residential staff who are poorly trained may fail to see connections between their attitude toward disabled children and the children's well being. I still come across care staff, teaching staff in residential schools and social workers who are too willing to laugh at and openly discuss the shortcomings of the children in their care, for no better reason than to make themselves feel better.

The steady drip-drip of being belittled increases the risk that children place a low value on themselves, and the likelihood that they will comply with adult wishes, even when the attention they receive is exploitative and abusive.

Risk is also reduced if children have higher self-esteem, and are able to say no. I stated in *Children First* that it would be a sign of progress when BLISS symbolics boards had a 'piss off' symbol, which view I still hold, but it also needs the confidence to use it (Middleton 1992). Disabled children need education, like other children, about their body, what its parts are called, what the slang words for penis are, and what is OK and what is not. They need to be educated about not having to keep secrets about sexual behaviour, and about what is acceptable in private and what is not. This is particularly important for children who require help with intimate personal care. We know that currently disabled children, especially those with learning disabilities, are less likely to receive education about sex and sexuality. Despite this, Ruth Marchant and Marcus Page strongly assert that even children with multiple disablilities can distinguish between touching which is directly related to care and that which is sexually motivated (Marchant and Page 1992).

They need to learn the importance of not talking to strangers and to understand what 'stranger' means. It can be confusing for a child if its mother persists in greeting her partner with 'Hello, Stranger' but happily jumps into taxi cabs with men she has never met before. Earlier chapters have discussed the effects of a segregated life experience, and the illusory protection which disabled children receive. Ignorance is not bliss: it is dangerous. Disabled children may relate to adults in a more compliant manner than non-disabled children in order to secure affection. Adult survivors have described how their limited life experience meant they were unaware that their abusive childhood was not normal (Morris 1995).

2. Managing Risk

An understanding of the above issues will help the social worker assess the risk to a particular child, in order to take protective action or to allocate resources, including the social worker's own time. Managing risk is an attempt to achieve a reasonable balance between the perceived dangers and the disadvantages for the child in terms of lost opportunities, restrictions on freedom or family break-up.

I reached the conclusion many years ago in working with old people that it is not only impossible entirely to legislate away all risk, but that attempting it may have undesirable consequences (Middleton 1981). The reassurance that reduced risk may offer to families or to professionals can be at the expense of the person being protected. With old people it threatened their preferred life-style, freedom of movement and privacy. With children overemphasis on protection can reduce opportunities to learn through exploration and experimentation, stunt their ability to deal with difficult or new situations and limit their play. It is probable that the widespread practice of driving children everywhere to avoid the dangers of abduction threatens their physical health unless some other regular exercise is substituted. Removal from home may prevent abuse but can have high emotional costs.

Risk assessment is a fashionable concept and there have been a number of attempts to create mechanistic devices to assist the process, including the use of computer programmes. These involve totting up a range of predictive indicators and allocating a score. These may be superficially attractive to departments seeking to make assessment a faster and more consistent process, but they are not really assessment in the sense of making analytical judgements.

The reliance on predicative indicators of risk carries dangers both of missing abuse in statistically low-risk families and being overly suspicious of others. As a result child protection enquiries focus disproportionately on parents who are on their own, poor, black, working class or who have low intelligence. Risk assessment results may be added to files and acted on in order to demonstrate the existence of a rational process and to watch the worker's back in a critical environment, whereas more accurate assessment might well be based on much less tangible factors, such as the social worker's judgement, the parents' credibility or the eyes of the child.

There is no easy formula. Getting the full picture is less like taking a photograph than doing a jigsaw when you've lost the lid to the box: the scene does not emerge all at once, the significant bits may not fit in until late and other people may well have some of the vital pieces. It is insufficient simply to add up indicators of risk. The process involves both the gathering of information and using it intelligently. Risk assessment means weighing the importance and relevance of risk factors within a particular family at a particular time.

Social workers have to make professional judgements about the level of risk by evaluating the extent of stress on a family, their ability to handle it and their own level of concern about the child. Observation is a key skill. The level of trust between social worker and family is crucial to how much will be openly discussed. Nothing is foolproof. The social worker will combine instinct, experience, the family's previous history and the family's own assessment and, before acting on any conclusion of their own, will consult with others.

Assessing risk should not be an alternative to providing support. It is quite unethical to test out a family's ability to care or to cope by subjecting them to avoidable pressure or the child to needless risk. It really does not matter whether someone would have abused a child if they did not receive a family aide, nor should people be put in the position of having to threaten to hit a child unless they receive a service. This means addressing the popular wisdoms that believe that the only way to secure, say, a day nursery place is to abuse your child. In those authorities where this is actually true some very serious thinking needs to be undertaken about cause and effect.

3. Action to help abused children

If prevention fails, social workers have to be prepared to act. It is not someone else's responsibility. For some disabled children, this means learning to communicate by means other than speech, or to work with an interpreter. For some reason, the former is a major paralysing factor for social workers: the single most common reason given to me for not wanting to get involved. Ruth Marchant and Marcus Page (1992) point out that in their experience it is police and social services interviewers who show greater visible anxiety than disabled children.

It reflects our self-consciousness as adults, but it is deeply dehumanising for children who may attribute the worker's anxiety to them or to their behaviour. I can recommend a sense of humour; most children can understand the difference between laughing at them and laughing at yourself. Children respond much better to adults who try to communicate than those who through arrogance or embarrassment pretend to understand. This is not to suggest it is not intensely frustrating, especially when the child is clearly distressed.

It should also perhaps be noted that some disabled children will use the difficulties in communication as a joke, exaggerate the problems or deliberately misbehave, even when the situation as the worker sees it is serious. They may do this to delay and gain more time and attention from a worker they like, or to prolong the discomfort of one they don't, or just because they think it is funny. In doing this they are simply being children, but I know that some adults find it hard to recognise or to deal with.

Helen Westcott and Merry Cross (1995) argue that adults often believe they cannot communicate with disabled children, and that this is a self fulfilling prophecy. All children need a means of communication. Establishing this should not have to wait until problems arise. This strengthens the argument in favour of retaining an existing social worker with a family after suspicion of abuse arises, since the means of communication should already be established.

The social work role involves either establishing a relationship of trust with the child directly, or ensuring that they have that level of trust with someone. This is vital whether or not any abuse is suspected. The child should feel safe enough to tell. This means knowing that they will not be blamed, but believed, and that something will be done. (This does not mean making false promises!) These three conditions can be established around issues other than abuse, and should reflect a consistent approach to the child as she grows. If children are confident in the good parts of their lives, they are more likely to report when something goes wrong. Once a social worker has the trust of a child she can assist in communications with others, such as the police, if that becomes necessary.

It helps if the social worker takes the decision to interview a child separately. Some children will not want their parents involved in the interview often for complex reasons, but find it hard to say so. Many disabled children blame themselves for the fact that the abuse is happening and fear the consequences of this 'bad behaviour' being known to their parents. Others are so steeped in guilt about the trouble they already cause their parents that they do not wish to add any further to their burdens.

There are good reasons not to involve parents when interviewing children about abuse, even when they are not directly under suspicion. Children will almost always be aware of the effect their story is having on their parent, and the presence of the parent is bound to affect what is said, however unwittingly. Parents are likely to be shocked both at the existence of the abuse and by the child's inability to share their distress with them, as well as having to deal with their own failure to protect. Their needs have to be dealt with separately rather than allowed to complicate or divert the interview or intrude into the child's time. The child may not know whether or not non-abusing parents approve of what is going on. The child and parents both require help to talk about, address and adjust their feelings.

More obviously if a child has been threatened with unpleasant consequences for 'telling' they will need to feel safe to share both what is happening, and what they believe will happen if they share information. Social workers need to give honest answers if trust is to be maintained on a long-term basis: there may well be unpleasant consequences of taking action to deal with abuse and the child needs to reach a realistic understanding of what these may be.

It is important not to lose sight of the fact that children who are being abused are damaged and experiencing emotional pain, and that this will be reflected in their communication with the worker. Children who describe sexual abuse often do so in very flat emotional terms which may convey the wrong impression to an insensitive interviewer, but which may mask very deep hurt. A disabled child may need to convey emotions in a different way, and the worker should be conscious of their difficulty in trying to convey a sense of what is happening and how it feels using communication techniques which may be clumsy and which may themselves create barriers.

It is not enough simply to wait for a child to communicate. Behaviour which may indicate abuse should always be logged, even though its significance may not be apparent until later, or until it is enhanced by other facts from fellow professionals or the family itself. It is sometimes difficult to separate possible indicators of abuse from factors relating to the disability. Both bruising and overt sexualised behaviour may be confusing in their causality, for example. It is common to blame the disability for every physical or behavioural difference, and such stereotyping is unhelpful.

There are a multitude of reasons why some parents abuse their own children. Some have unrealistic expectations of parenthood and of their children. This may reflect their age, or their own experiences of being parented, or the lack of support available to them. Children crying or being dirty or disobedient are behaving quite normally as children, and yet may be seen as not rewarding their parents, or even as being hostile to them. A disabled child may not grow or achieve at the expected rate. Some adults enjoy or prefer sexual relationships with children, see their own children as legitimate and easy targets and may see it as an expression of love.

Where a child is disabled, support from relatives and friends may be less forthcoming and less readily accepted, for a range of reasons more fully described in Chapter 6. Professional support is also harder to come by. Parents may be loath to complain about a child whom others see as an object of pity.

Given the initial premise that most parents do not want to injure their children, and that risks to children may arise out of stress, tiredness, or loss of control, the parent should be encouraged to explore and talk about these problems, as part of normal family life. This is more likely if they believe that the social worker intends to help, rather than punish them or remove the child. At present the reality is that many parents see the social worker as a threat and are loath to ask for help. The evidence is that most instances of child abuse are relatively mild, yet the service is designed around the minority at the heavy end (DOH 1995). Social workers with an existing relationship with a family have a greater chance of helping the majority of potentially mild abusers. Indeed the intervention of a child protection specialist, who may be scared or ignorant about disability issues, could add to the stress a family feels and will almost certainly convey lack of confidence to the child.

There will be some cases where the child is at serious risk and trapped in a no-win scenario. I have noticed with some degree of dismay that this is the point at which many of the guides to child abuse and disability skip from 'investigation and assessment' onto 'helping survivors', without addressing any of the very difficult decisions that must occur in between. Social workers left to find a way through this minefield should perhaps remind themselves that the responsibility for the abuse is not theirs, and that some situations are impossible to fix! The task becomes one of damage limitation, and requires confidence and commitment to finding the best way through for the child. The only appropriate response may be removal of either the child or perpetrator from home. While pressing for the latter, the chances are that it will be the child who suffers the double indignity of abuse and removal. If the abuse is physical even parents who cause serious injury are likely to feel bad about it, but there comes a point where the actual safety of the child has to come first and efforts to heal second.

The fact that the child is disabled should make no difference to the responsibility on the local authority to seek an appropriate placement, bearing in mind the age, gender and race of the child as well as the particular requirements around the impairment. This is not easy, but it remains vital to retain a commitment to childcare principles and not simply accommodate the child within an institution which can cope physically with the disability. Social workers from a disability background will find themselves learning on their feet as they discover the reactions of a child within the care system, and are advised to contact experienced colleagues as they help the child to negotiate it. Most of the issues will be the same as they are for a non-disabled child away from home.

Children will clearly be feeling very vulnerable at this time. There will be mixed and complex feelings and continuity of contact with a trusted worker is essential. They may blame themselves, possibly focusing on a characteristic such as race or disability or on some other perceived failure.

Foster care, like that of natural parents, is usually safe, but it is unwise to make assumptions. Abuse occurs in foster homes for the same raft of reasons that it occurs within the natural family. Nor can the opportunistic sexual abuser be ruled out: applying to foster disabled children may seem like an easy way to achieve sexual gratification, given the dearth of applicants for this task and the low value put on the safety of disabled children. Removal is clearly legally much simpler, but carries similar issues for the child, especially if the placement has been long-term. There is also ample scope for conflict between workers who approved the foster carers and those who accuse. I have encountered some Family Placement Workers who maintain a complete mental block on the possibility of 'their' foster carers being possible abusers. This can be a particular feature within voluntary organisations which rescue disabled children and whose fund-raising ability may be affected if there is any doubt about the saintliness of their carers.

The shortage of foster carers is a national phenomenon more keenly felt with disabled children. There are policy issues here, given the current practice in many authorities to maintain separate lists of foster carers for disabled and non-disabled children. All potential foster carers should be helped toward an acceptance of their role as including caring for disabled children. Much of their reluctance will reflect prejudice and ignorance, as well as the more justifiable fear of the lack of support they may receive.

Finally, services for disabled survivors of abuse are as limited as those of prevention and protection. This is a vicious circle which diminishes the quality of child protection services due to the lack of feedback into the system about what works and what does not. Developing services for survivors does not have to follow slavishly the therapeutic models from the United States, which focus on victimhood (even where it is called 'survival'). Groupwork can aim to raise awareness and restore self-esteem by directing anger outwards and blame where it rightfully belongs: with perpetrators. While there are arguments for groups of all disabled survivors, I am inclined toward mixed groups, which can help disabled victims to recognise that non-disabled children are also abused, and that their disability is not the cause.

This is an area of work where social workers will come across many individuals suffering distressing and long-term ill effects. This can be demoralising. It is worth remembering that they do not represent the whole of the picture: it is possible to overcome both the physical and emotional effects of being abused and enjoy positive relationships.

Professional and organisational issues

Whether or not they see their specialism as disability or childcare, social workers all need to be aware of the possibility of abuse and their agencies' systems for responding to it. These should be triggered regardless of the disability or non-disability of the child. All social workers should be trained in child protection, and familiar with the help and advice that is available to them. Those responsible for contracting for services need to ensure workers in service agencies employ trained staff. Child protection is also a glaring gap in the education and training of most of the therapists whom disabled children might encounter (Russell 1994).

There are considerable tensions around the best way to organise child protection work. These are surfacing more and more as recognition is given to the need, and right, of disabled children to protection. There are a number of models being operated at present, changes in approach having been generated by the Children Act and the introduction in some authorities of specialist teams for disabled children within children's services. There are issues here both for individual workers in opting for or being allocated certain areas of responsibility, and structural issues about the organisation of the department.

It is not my intention in the next section to be overprescriptive: these are early days and there are undoubtedly a number of routes to get to the same place. The following offers some reflections based on a questionnaire survey about the organisation of child protection for disabled children, and notes from follow up meetings. Respondents were social workers from twelve local authorities.

Social workers are coming into the work of protecting disabled children from two different directions: from existing child protection services which need to expand their remit to cover disabled children; and from disability workers, some of whom may have no previous experience of childcare work at all.

Despite the hostile culture in which they must operate child protection workers from the range of disciplines involved largely still maintain both a commitment to children and to cooperation across agency and professional boundaries. Such cooperative working practice is being rapidly eroded in other areas because of the imposition of the divisive values of the marketplace. Indeed child protection seems to be one area of social work where the essentially competitive pressures of the market economy are being resisted by practitioners and where the artificial divisions of purchaser/provider are being challenged. I am unsure whether the multidisciplinary culture which operates at practitioner level is the result of professional resistance to the accountants, or whether its preexistence is enabling people to withstand the pressures to fragment. These days it does seem that professionals from all agencies are more disenchanted with their own organisations than they are frustrated by professional differences.

While working across agencies is clearly sensible, it can serve to set child protection workers apart from other childcare workers within social services departments in a way which is ultimately unhelpful to families. This separation seems to follow external pressures for a high-profile, 'investigate, catch, prosecute' style of working rather than reflecting a considered response by a local authority to reducing the incidence of abuse.

There is a myth that working with families who abuse is essentially different and requires different workers from generic childcare work. The underlying principles are no different: nor are the skills that are required to be effective in helping people and situations to change. There is no sound professional argument for bringing in a different worker at a point in a 'case' where its bureaucratic status changes from childcare to child protection. There may be sound arguments for additional professional involvement, or increased supervision for the worker, but *automatically* changing worker as a matter of policy means that the organisation is using two levels of childcare workers, only one of which is deemed competent in recognising and dealing with potential and actual abuse. This is professionally unacceptable and creates a status gulf between childcare and child protection. If the former are also designated as a disability team the gulf is potentially even wider. Ruth Marchant and Marcus Page (1992) identified this unhelpful gap some years ago as a contributing factor to the vulnerability of disabled children. This gap continues to exist and is being coupled with some strange double-think. Some authorities are developing separate procedures for child protection where the child is disabled. In some cases this involves an existing worker from a disability team retaining the case where the suspected abuse is to a disabled child, but passing it on to a child protection team if a non-disabled sibling is thought to be the victim.

There may be good reasons for changing worker if the relationship with the family breaks down, or in long and complex cases. At the end of the day the competency, commitment and attitude of the worker and their approach to the family are more important than their official designation.

> *I have some limited investigation experience where the children have been on my caseload and have had learning disabilities, but I would rather not be involved in this area on a regular basis*
>
> (Questionnaire respondent)

It seems fairly clear that a significant number of social workers who consider themselves disability specialists do not want to become involved in child protection. It is widely regarded as a distinct specialism from which it is possible to stay apart. I have already indicated that I cannot go along with this separation of responsibility. Just as a parent has responsibility both to care for and protect her child, so a social worker has to carry the same range of responsibility. This is not to deny that many social services departments are not organised along these lines, and do separate responsibility where disabled children are concerned. Before discussing organisational issues it seems essential to explore the reasons why so many disability specialists do not want to engage in protecting children.

First, child protection work is scary. It has a frightening image as a 'damned if you do, damned if you don't' area of work, and it can be frightening in reality to know that a child's life may depend on getting it right. It generates a great deal of anxiety which can increase the risk of ill-considered decisions so that the risk of a bad experience is high for a worker on their first excursion into the area. Since the child they are involved with is disabled, there is also a high probability that the support they will receive is less than for those workers in child protection teams who have been specially trained and have ready access to expert colleagues or supervision.

Social workers used to the helping culture usual in working with disabled children or adults may not be attracted by child protection work because of its macho image and the culture of blame which surrounds it. It is widely perceived as a job which involves following the rules, heavy investigative work, standing up in court and keeping a great many detailed records. The blame culture is a very real problem which handicaps workers in operating in partnership, or in acting creatively, and requires addressing at a policy level if child protection is to move on. Blame extends beyond the social services and pervades their relationship with parents who see social workers as a threat. This leads to disability workers being able to make conceptual separations between the nice relationship they enjoy with families and the nasty investigative intrusions of the child protection worker. One social worker described how she had to visit families afterwards to 'soothe and smooth'.

The avoidance of responsibility for protecting the child is therefore justified as being threatening to the relationship with the parents. Such an attitude is not really tenable, given the primary duty to protect the child, and it also begs serious questions not only about the quality of the relationship, but what the social worker sees as her purpose in visiting the family.

If it is true that the disability social worker does enjoy a good relationship with parents, she should be in the best position to find out what is going on within the family, to assess any risk to the child, and to offer appropriate support. In some areas co-working has become the pattern. This can be an excellent compromise if the workers are there to share expertise and aid communication. It is less attractive where one worker plays the nasty investigator while the other plays the family helper. This is divisive and leaves the family with a lack of confidence in the worker who remains with them. It is entirely appropriate to combine the role of discovering what is happening in a family with that of helping. Indeed, a family is more likely to cooperate in an investigation if it is seen as an attempt to help.

It is possible that social workers, and other professionals find it hard to adjust their priorities if the original reason for their contact with the family was not alleged abuse. The Children Act's emphasis on partnership with parents should not be allowed to divert attention from the responsibility to assess risk, and investigate where there is any reasonable cause for suspicion. This responsibility to investigate should be complemented with the responsibility to support and offer help. Any idea that child protection work is simply about catching and punishing is unhelpful to the child. The local authority carries the broader responsibility to train all its staff who deal with children to be alert to the possibilities of abuse, and to be aware of the supportive systems which should be in place to respond.

Lack of adequate training is cited as a reason for wishing to avoid child protection work. Where social workers in disability teams are denied access to child protection training, a feeling of incompetence might be both real and justified. This is an organisational issue, which is rooted in discriminatory approaches to disabled children as requiring a different level of service, but it is probably also true to say that many workers collude in their own ignorance rather than actively challenging their employers to include them in training.

There are understandable reasons for workers not to wish to change the nature of their task. Many place a high value on aspects of their work which they believe, rightly or wrongly, will be lost if they are expected to undertake child protection. Many feel they are allowed to operate relatively autonomously, and talk about a freedom from controlling management which allows them to work creatively and flexibly. It is a sad reflection that this is rarely expressed positively as experience of enabling management, but of a freedom derived from undertaking work that is unimportant to the organisation. Management that does not interfere is also distant and uncaring but, while self-motivating individuals can thrive in such a culture, it is clearly not appropriate for child protection. The big question is 'Can child protection managers be enabling?' I have encountered a number who are keen to convince me that they can, and I believe them. However, the senior childcare managers who attend conferences aimed at social workers with disabled children are in all probability not a representative sample!!

There is a role for self motivating and creative staff within child protection. Indeed, I would go so far as to say that it would be hard adequately to protect disabled children without them. Creativity and flexibility are needed to get to know families, communicate with children, offer support in an acceptable way and actively manage risk where there are no easy fall-back positions in terms of residential or foster placements. Child protection managers may or may not need to alter their style, but they clearly need to look at their image.

> *We were started on reduced resources, which are likely to reduce further, without clarity as to our roles and purpose....Consequently we are deluged with work and now waiting for senior management decisions as to which type of work will be dealt with by the specialist team, and what will happen to the rest....At present we are not approved for Child Protection investigations, but crazy though this might seem we are working toward becoming so. This is mostly because of the lack of appropriate service currently offered....Lack of disability awareness and fundamental non understanding of the rights and needs of children with Disabilities make it imperative that we develop the expertise required, and be able to share it with colleagues from other teams.*
>
> (extract from a Letter from a Team Manager)

The Children Act has seen the introduction of specialist teams for disabled children in many local authorities, and others are in the process of considering their establishment. Some of these specialist disability teams touch no child protection work at all, some deal with all cases, while others like the team above, are working towards taking responsibility. In practice, much may depend on the attitude of the team manager and their own confidence and interest in managing child protection.

This leaves a range of fudged strategies in between. There are those who keep the case if they were working with the family at the time, and if the abuse relates to the disabled child, but do not pick up new referrals relating to abuse; nor, significantly, do they deal with the suspected abuse if it is to a non-disabled child! This two-tier system has no professional justification.

Some organisations are also separating by type of disability, with children with learning disabilities being dealt with separately from other disabled children. This all adds up to a disturbingly complex morass in which responses are distinguished both by type of abuse: physical or sexual; and by category of child: non-disabled, learning disabled, physically disabled. If emotional, medical, institutional, financial and racial abuse were to be included this could potentially result in a whole range of specialist responses! It is clearly already possible in some authorities to have a number of social workers investigating the same family, as well as interpreters, police officers and medical personnel.

In addition, management lines of accountability are confused. Many social workers were unable to tell me which manager was responsible for the protection of disabled children and made nervous statements such as 'hopefully they will liaise'.

An alarming number of social workers reported an absence of written policies about the abuse of disabled children, or a stated assumption that procedures as they were currently written were automatically appropriate. This is unlikely to be the case, since in the absence of any serious thought such policies will fail to take account of the particular vulnerabilities to which disabled children are exposed or the wider range of skills necessary to provide a protection service. One particularly worrying response noted that in the absence of any organisational guidelines the policy would depend on the worker involved on the day.

Key issues

There are a number of key issues emerging which should be borne in mind when setting up services to protect disabled children. These may seem obvious, but the evidence points to their not being considered in many authorities.

- It is discriminatory not to provide the same level of child protection expertise and trained staff to disabled children as is available to non-disabled children.
- Good support for vulnerable families will help prevent the incidence of child abuse.
- Developing services at home obviates the need to remove children.
- Disabled children are more vulnerable to abuse than non-disabled children, from a wider range of possible perpetrators and in a wider range of settings.
- Procedures designed with non-disabled children in mind will not be sufficient to protect disabled children.
- Management accountability should be clear.
- A worker who can communicate with a disabled child and has the trust of a family has a better chance of discovering the truth about what is happening in a family than a new worker.
- Disability social workers are put off child protection work by its image, which is also intimidating for families.

The key to change?

Despite much of the gloom and doom described above, it is also true that the abuse of disabled children is much more likely to be an agenda item now for local authorities than it was even a few years ago. There was virtually no discussion of the subject when I wrote *Children First* during 1990–91, nor much in the way of reading. There is now an increasingly wide variety of publications and training materials available. Social services departments are discussing the issue and many are making changes to policy and practice. It is important that this is well informed not only to ensure that the child protection service offered is appropriate, but also because it will influence all services for disabled children. Child protection and childcare for disabled children are not separable.

The current lack of suitable alternatives to being looked after at home for many disabled children has paralysed social services into inaction when abuse is suspected. It should act as an incentive to departments to develop new support services at home, rather than slavishly following protection patterns which rely on rescue into residential or foster care. This is in accord with the Children Act requirement to maintain children within their own families and communities where possible. In achieving the means to protect disabled children without their removal to institutional care, local authorities will be improving their childcare practices for all children. As such taking children away from home could become a last resort used only in very exceptional circumstances.

Much abuse of disabled children takes place outside the home in educational, medical and care settings. It is very clearly the responsibility of the purchaser, care manager or social worker who is accessing these services on behalf of a family to ensure that they are safe. Social services have a clear lead responsibility for the welfare of disabled children, and this includes investigating any situation where there is a suggestion of abusive practice. There are obvious responsibilities for those workers directly involved in the provision of care, and managerial ones to encourage and support a sense of responsibility among workers for the welfare and safety of the child which overrides loyalty to colleagues who abuse. In both these ways responsibility for the safety of the child is inseparable from responsibility for her care. Good practice will improve both safety and other aspects of care.

This truth applies no less in the child's own home. Good parenting can be encouraged by easing stress, giving information and offering support, including financial support. Increasing a sense of worth in the parents by an emphasis on the equal rights of the disabled child in society is a longer term goal, since disabled children are clearly not yet valued equally. This makes them more vulnerable to abuse, at home and outside it. It is another one of those vicious circles! In this case it may be easier to break into the cycle by demonstrating a clear commitment to protection, which in turn sends out a message that disabled children matter just as much, and that the social services are committed to working toward an equitable child protection service.

This message and the changes in practice resulting from it would also influence the quality and value put on the whole range of work with disabled children and offer a key to improved practice.

Chapter 5
Easy as ABC? The Social Work Role

Social work is about making things happen. It is also about releasing and fostering feeling and emotion in others: not for its own sake, but to help healing, to gird for action, to develop commitment to change, to cope with disappointment and to enjoy success.

Chapter 1 examined welfare services for disabled children from a structural perspective, and concluded that the Children Act was failing in its intention to integrate services for disabled children. This chapter seeks to explore the role of social work as a professional activity. Social work roles might be a more accurate description, since there are a number of ways in which a social worker may relate to a disabled child and family. As activities they are clearly distinct, and although they are not mutually exclusive, they do sometimes make uneasy companions. Care management and advocacy are one obviously ill-suited pair. Other roles are assessment, counselling, child protection, family work, facilitating, networking, groupwork and political action.

This chapter explores the new roles of assessment, brokerage and care management and attempts to construct a child-centred approach to such work. It then addresses the question of whether social work with disabled children is anything more than assessment and service brokerage and, if so, what else might it be? What has social work got to offer?

One obvious point is that social work with disabled children involves working with their families, preferably in partnership. Social work with disabled children is a minority interest and a difficult option. It involves getting involved in complex family dynamics and engaging with highly charged emotions from children, families and other professionals.

There is no such thing as a blueprint for practice: social work is an art, not a science. It can be emotionally draining. Employers may not always recognise this, nor provide appropriate support, and social workers are well advised to ensure they organise their own back-up!

Ruth Marchant and Marcus Page describe how difficult professionals can find it to establish rapport with children who have multiple disabilities and who cannot communicate by methods familiar to them (Marchant and Page 1992).

Adults unfamiliar with disability will experience emotional reactions to disabled children which are best acknowledged. Most able-bodied adults grow up in a world in which disabled children are hidden, unfamiliar and scary. The reality of understanding that a disabled child is experiencing abuse and communicating their distress is hard, particularly where the worker can see no way to 'fix it'. Ruth Marchant and Marcus Page speculate that this kind of pain may be accentuated because of the degree of concentration required to communicate as well as by the fact of the child's vulnerability.

Social workers need to be conscious of their own feelings and have the ability to keep them out of the way where they are unhelpful. There may be unresolved issues around disability in their own lives, or in those of their families, of which the social worker needs to be aware.

It may seem hard then, that the work involved is not highly regarded by the social services department, nor by the public at large. Support is less likely from colleagues either in terms of time out, listening space or advice. Career prospects are poor. All these hygiene factors discourage workers from making the effort and drive them into areas of work which are better regarded. This is not good news for disabled children, where continuity of contact over many years has long been known to be a valued resource (Glendinning 1983).

These are matters for a range of people to address, from journalists and television stars to politicians and educators, when they recognise what harm their own disabilism may be effecting within society.

More immediately, social services managers should be addressing issues of status and support within their organisations, so the latter is targeted where the work is demanding and complex rather than high profile and highly paid. Until such shifts are made to value those staff who work with disabled children the service they receive will continue to suffer.

All these issues are largely outside an individual social worker's control and it may be tempting to shrug shoulders and wait for the world to change. However, there is a case for putting social work's house in order rather than occupying an illusory moral high ground and expecting everyone else to look at themselves. Social workers have been guilty of not always being clear and confident about their own roles and contributions: it is a broad and changing profession. The rest of this chapter explores both the new ABC of social work and then revisits some more familiar areas.

Assessment, brokerage and care management: the new ABC of social work

The tasks of assessment, brokerage and care management constitute the new role of social work, and indeed of other professional helpers, on the purchaser side of the purchaser/provider split. It is not easy for such a divide to operate at practitioner level, but workers are increasingly expected to try, and this chapter swims with that particular tide. Social work as a service in itself is considered later.

Assessment...

Before it acquired its capital A, assessment used to mean simply making an analysis or appraisal of a situation. Exercising judgement was something that could either be done swiftly by glancing around a room or into a person's eyes, or take considerably longer. Reassessment was ongoing! It has developed by its inclusion in recent legislation and government guidance into something much more formal and mysterious. All the same, the original concept was not wrong and it is helpful to bear in mind that assessment should be about analysis and appraisal. The requirement to think is often lost sight of in the rush for scientific assessment tools, pseudo-psychological formula and more comprehensive methods of gathering and storing data. Assessment is a means to an end, not an end in itself. It follows that any documentation is only useful if it serves the end. It can have no intrinsic value of its own: nor is there any merit in collecting data that are not relevant.

Government guidance on assessment has been interpreted with too much emphasis on standardised data and quick fixes. Professional judgement has been devalued in the face of managerially driven formats and consequently managerial control. It is because of these organisational trends that this chapter intends to go back and restate basics, in the depressing belief that some people will be entrusted with assessment as a task without necessarily ever having been exposed to them. First, though, it is perhaps necessary to note that these trends are not mindless, but reflect the fact that ambitions of organisations are very different from those who seek to carry out a professional assessment. Similar pressures to conform were exerted on educational psychologists trying to undertake assessments of educational need under the old 1981 Education Act, where the education departments that employed them did not wish to see Statements of Need which would require extra financial commitment.

Why do organisations assess? It is clear from the efforts made to devise and introduce assessment forms, procedures and dedicated staff that this is an organisationally valued activity, provided it is carried out in the right way for the organisation. It is increasingly necessary to justify expenditure or lack of expenditure, and auditors like to see solid evidence of systems, within which there are always logical and formula-based outcomes for set inputs. Auditors, chairs of complaints panels and judicial reviewers tend not to like matters left to individual circumstance, professional judgement or negotiation. Rather they are interested in set criteria and written rules. Impressive looking assessment tools may not assist the analytical process one jot, but they are valued as evidence that something scientific is going on. The system looks equitable and can therefore be very reasonably used by the organisation to justify rationing.

Organisations do not want to be told that what passes as rational criteria can depend very much on the value judgements of the individual ticking the boxes, and even on the time of day the assessment was performed.

Not only can pseudo-scientific assessment tools be used to justify rationing, they act as rationing devices in themselves: they put people off. Social workers who get to someone's house, open a bulging briefcase and produce a large form dehumanise the process and keep control a long way from the service user and, incidentally, from themselves. Social workers who are interested in the promotion of the rights of individuals face a very real dilemma when asked to act as a rationer of service, since their professional judgement will almost certainly conflict with the role placed on them by the organisation. Small wonder that authorities seeking to limit expenditure are tempted to employ unqualified staff to conduct assessments of need.

Once completed, the assessment forms can be used by the organisation to compare resource allocation across different professionals, and so rule out idiosyncratic behaviour. To put it another way: professionals are disempowered by being hedged in by bureaucratic hurdles, rules and criteria. Was all this the government's intention? Not on the face of, at least.

The overt expectations of government are noteworthy, and social work may have felt less cynical if such aims were adequately funded and genuinely meant. While it is difficult to agree with them in entirety, they are useful concepts which are not incompatible with sound social work.

Care Management and Assessment: The Practitioners Guide is probably the most accessible source (Social Services Inspectorate 1991). This emphasises four major themes:

1. Services should be fitted to need, not vice versa. The service outcome, in other words, should not be pre-supposed in the initial responses;
2. Assessing need should be separated from the delivery of service;
3. A revision of organisational structures and change of managerial attitude and approach are needed;
4. The empowerment of users and carers is a key concept.

The Social Services Inspectorate adds its own standards for assessment in the 1991 Guide 'Getting the Message Across'

Assessment should:

> *– recognise that some users may be the best assessors of their own needs and solutions*
> *– consider the needs and strengths of individuals in the context of their everyday lives*
> *– be separate from a decision about allocation of services*
> *– strike a balance between invading privacy and obtaining sufficient information*
> *– recognise the rights of carers to a separate assessment*
> *– be ethnically and culturally sensitive.*
>
> (Social Services Inspectorate 1991)

Most of these expectations are reinforced in the Guidance to the Children Act which stresses that people should not be assessed to fit existing services, but that services should be adapted to meet need. Social services are instructed to provide information about services and about the assessment procedures that have been put in place to determine need. Key concepts are partnership with parents and children, listening to children, and not making assumptions based on categories of disability.

The quarrel with these concepts rests not on the notion of a needs led service, but on the understanding of need that underpins it. We could spend many pages discussing what is meant by need, and I do not intend to get bogged down, but we might usefully compare the government definition with an understanding informed by anti-oppressive practice.

The government tells us, rightly, that need is a complex concept which has been analysed in a variety of different ways, but as far as they are concerned it means:

> *a shorthand for the requirements of individuals to enable them to achieve, maintain or restore an acceptable level of social independence or quality of life, as defined by the particular care agency or authority*
> (Social Services Inspectorate 1991: p12)

The sting is in the tail: need is relative, and locally defined.

An anti-oppressive stance would hold that a person's need relates not simply to requirements to *'achieve, maintain or restore'* but is, crucially, about the removal of artificial obstacles and barriers that prevent or hinder children from achieving normal goals related to their age and ability. In fact, it might be more helpful to delete the concept of need altogether, given its tendency to be professionally determined, and substitute rights or aspirations.

The basic needs of disabled children are no different from those of any other child. All children need (or have a right to) warmth, security, food, to be loved, to play, to learn, to grow, to take risks, to make friends and explore relationships, and to be free from abuse and exploitation. The concept of 'special need' has been extremely misleading in promoting a notion that disabled children somehow have different needs from the rest of children. What is different is the barriers which relate specifically to disabled children and make them 'special'. Alternatively, the usual means of meeting the need which is appropriate to non-disabled children may not help a child with a particular impairment. Disability is made worse for some children by the absence of *appropriate* artificial aids. For example, when being fed a disabled child may simply require a spoon of a different shape or made from different material. If this is available, the disability may disappear or become merely an inconvenience. It is worth remembering that many widely used artificial aids are not considered stigmatic, nor their users considered to be disabled because of reliance on them: glasses for short sight are an obvious example, but we might also cite toothbrushes, forks or lightbulbs.

In weighing options against each other for meeting needs, or securing rights, social workers should be mindful of the normal ways of meeting them, within whatever family or cultural setting, and then try to ascertain why that solution is not available for the particular disabled child.

An example might help. All children want to play and mix with other children. Non-disabled children achieve this by visiting friends' homes, playing in the street or at school, going to playgroups, joining Cubs and Brownies, or youth clubs. A disabled child might find problems being involved in these activities for a range of reasons. The attitudes of the parents of non-disabled children may discourage them from mixing with disabled children. Parents of a disabled child may not invite other children around for fear their child may be harmed by too rough play or by unkind remarks. The disabled child may attend a different school, at some distance from home, so that both child and parent have different acquaintances. Friends from special school are harder to keep in touch with because of distance, transport and communication problems. Long periods of hospitalisation may disturb patterns of friendship from developing near home. Access to playgroups, Cubs, Brownies and so on may be difficult if the organisers or buildings are not equipped to cope with a disabled child. Playing out in the street, a calculated risk for all children, may seem even more so for a disabled child.

Some of these difficulties are more intractable than others, but the stock 'solutions' of isolated, adult-orientated play at home, or special day care, will not fulfil the child's need to experience a normal childhood. Some difficulties are illusory. The idea that disabled children are harmed by mixing with non-disabled children is one: they are no more at risk than any child is from another. Children do bully and can be cruel, and will pick on any source of difference in this, but they will not discriminate particularly on disability. Any odd characteristic will do nicely: height, weight, short sight, stutter, strange accent, ginger hair, freckles, spots, black skin, living on a farm, boring shoes.…I am not for a moment condoning bullying, nor denying that it is deeply unpleasant to be on the receiving end of it, but it is part of life and does not go away with adulthood. Learning to deal with it is as important a lesson for a disabled child as any other, perhaps more so. A disabled child who does not learn to live with non-disabled people will find life that much tougher to negotiate as an adult. It is also necessary to learn to cope with risk and to learn this with other children.

An assessment relating to a disabled child should not focus on the deficiency of the child, but on the barriers to their hopes and aspirations, within their own context. It follows that any assessment must first start with the aim of finding out what these hopes and aspirations might be.

The process of assessment is also available for us in government guidance! It makes it all sound very easy. The formula is as follows:

> *negotiate the scope of the assessment*
>
> *choose the setting*
>
> *clarify expectations*
>
> *promote partnership*
>
> *establish a relationship of trust*
>
> *assess need*
>
> *determine eligibility*
>
> *set priorities*
>
> *agree objectives*
>
> *record the assessment*
>
> (Social Services Inspectorate 1991)

Neither sticking to the above formula, nor arriving with a form to complete is going to cut much ice with most children. Clearly the assessment has to be age related and has to involve the parents or carers to a greater or lesser extent. The social worker needs to have sorted out what the assessment is all about. It will either be related to a particular issue or problem presented by the child or family, or a more general assessment initiated under some piece of legislation, such as for school leaving.

In offering the following 'stages of assessment' I am acutely aware of creating an undue focus on the process, which carries the danger of substituting one bureaucratic looking formula for another. This is not my intention. I can only emphasise that social workers, or others undertaking assessment, should understand it as an exercise with purpose and not simply a directionless conversation or interaction. This does not mean substituting set routines, or indulging in standardised questioning at the expense of open listening. All the stages offered below should be accompanied by time for both child and worker to reflect on what is being communicated and how it is being understood. The stages are not prescriptive, but offered as a logical and workable model. It is also worth emphasising, lest we invest too much in assessment, that all assessments have a limited shelf life, and are only useful in determining the next steps or phases of action. They should not be added to the file as life plans, or lasting determinants of the future. Understanding assessment this way makes the whole process less awesome.

Stage one: establishing a trusting relationship

Getting to know the child is the first and obvious step. This may not be easy given that the child may have been used to others answering for her and of not being expected to make decisions and choices of her own. Parents may assist or resist the social worker who wishes to deal with the child directly. In my experience, if it is clear that this is not intended to exclude them, most parents welcome it. Occasionally separate workers for child and parent help, usually for older children. Students and voluntary workers can be used very constructively in such cases.

The 'getting to know' phase will differ with the age of the child. Young children will not sit and answer questions and may need sneaking up on to some extent. This is no different to communicating with a non-disabled child. The skills of watching, observing, listening, reflecting back, checking out, empathising and recording are no different. Some things will take longer. Siblings are of enormous value in these situations, not only as additional information into the picture, but as informants whose view is both pertinent and candid. Children should be allowed, indeed encouraged to ask the questions, since these will more accurately express their concerns than those the social worker formulates, and should expect to get honest answers. The views and concerns of the child should be recorded as part of the assessment process. This not only helps in reaching decisions about action, but helps the growth of the relationship in enabling the social worker to read, reflect, and pick up themes after such a period of reflection.

It follows that social workers who are good at communicating with children will also be good at communicating with disabled children. If there are problems for such workers, they reflect their unease at dealing with the fact of disability. This may be prejudice or lack of confidence about the unfamiliar.

Many adults have grown up hidden from disability and have developed fears and prejudices about it. It is important that the worker gets it very clear in her own mind that she is required to exercise her social work skills, not act as a medical practitioner. Anything she needs to know about the disability, or about the method of communication, will come from the child herself, or from the family. It only takes an open mind, and a certain lack of inhibition. The latter is often the most difficult hurdle, especially since fumblings toward understanding are invariably in the public gaze of parent, carer or teacher. Like learning French, it takes a thick skin and a sense of humour. Meeting children half way using their method of communication is always appreciated, even if a translator is needed for the finer points!

Communicating with children is considered sufficient of an art in itself to merit whole books on the subject, and I do not propose to attempt a complete guide here. For those social workers who don't take to it naturally, a few points are worth emphasising:

Try and relax, or at least look relaxed. Get on the floor if you need to. Remember you are a stranger, and children are told, rightly, not to talk to strangers. As such you are at best a puzzle, at worse a threat. It is important not to rush. Children get on best with little known adults who let them set the pace and the agenda. The social worker may appear posh, smell funny, use long words or wear strange clothes. The child should be allowed to explore your unfamiliarity while safely on their familiar ground. It is always better to let the child occupy the space first, and not be disconcerted by finding a strange adult in their home. Not rushing is even more important where the child is from a different cultural, racial or class background and of a different gender.

Don't be too friendly. Remember how it felt to be smothered by large aunts and uncles who appeared annually on Boxing Day and wanted kissing?

Make use of the parents or siblings as advisers. If not consulted they may resort to the pleasant pastime of simply enjoying your discomfort.

For some children, attention from an adult may make them think they have done something wrong, and create fear.

Finally, be prepared to play. Use toys, pictures, computers, imaginary people and places. This is simply about building trust and making friends. Children fantasise as they play, and are not usually trying to communicate a shock revelation about real life.

Having established some trust, and started to know the family, the social worker can concentrate on undertaking an assessment.

Stage two: establishing the ground rules.
This means being clear either about what the problem is, if there is any, or what the point of assessment is at that particular time. In other words the reason for the assessment should be understood both by the child and the family. It may relate to school leaving, for example, or to a particular problem. The process may have been asked for by the family, or by the social services or another agency.

This part of the process might more positively be conceptualised as establishing aims, and reaching agreement about how they are to be achieved, who is to be involved, what documents are to be consulted, what form the recording is to take and who will get copies of whatever is written, taped or videotaped.

Stage three: find out what the individual or family wants
This means finding out what the family or individual actually wants, *not needs,* either in relation to the problem, or simply in the next stage of their life.

What is it that they actually aspire to for themselves, for the present and in the future? Disabled children often have plans for their future: in my experience very conventional, such as marriage and children. Asking disabled children what they want rarely results in unreasonable or widely impractical demands since they are conditioned to expect little from life.

What they want as a first choice may have to be tempered with what they will actually settle for, if there are less expensive or more easily available options for meeting the perceived need, but it is still good practice to find out what the preferred solution would be. It follows that the social worker has to be clear in their own mind of the difference between a want and a need. This is best done by ensuring that the family are expressing their own wishes and not simply choosing from a list of options imposed by the worker. Wants should not be constrained by preconceived ideas about what is available or reasonable to demand. It should be OK to express what they would really like, even if they believe it to be impossible to achieve. Doing this gives a sense of direction and purpose and an idea of the priorities of the family. There is no danger of artificially raising expectations if the questions are phrased appropriately. Such an open approach leaves freedom to explore possibilities that may not ever be considered if initial discussions are too closely confined.

Assessment should be of the situation, not simply of the child. It is important that the worker starts without pre-set assumptions. The most common pre-judgement relates to diagnosis which in itself is only a part of the picture. It may indicate little or nothing about level of impairment, nor of the prognosis for the future, and can tell nothing of personality or family circumstances. It is not helpful to start from a medical perspective. Children who have lived with a disabling condition for a while will be used to professionals who focus on it, and on the limitations it imposes. It may come as a surprise to them to experience a professional worker who wishes to focus on them as a person instead, and some older children can find this change of approach difficult at first.

Assessment should start from where the child is. What do they enjoy doing? What is their place in the family? How do they relate to their parents, step parents, siblings, grandparents and so on? For older children this is also about how they see their own life and their future. This exploration should widen to take in their experience of schooling, and their contacts within the community. Who are their friends?

If the child needs care, what exactly is needed? Who undertakes it? Is it appropriate to the child's age, gender, race? Is it considered safe? What are the child's fears? Are they real? How can they be allayed?

Stage four: resources

Stage four is to make yourself and the family aware of what resources are actually available and what can be engineered. This means resources in the widest possible meaning of the word: physical, emotional, spiritual, financial, family, statutory and voluntary services, community facilities, private organisations. Time needs to be spent in gathering data about the family, their friends and social networks as well as organisations operating in the area. There are advantages here for the experienced worker who knows her patch, not simply in terms of social services, but the community as a whole. In particular, it is useful to have knowledge of mainstream facilities that include, or could be encouraged to include, disabled children.

Once resources are identified they can be listed as possible options for achieving the aspirations, solving the problem or meeting the need identified earlier. It is important at this stage to list everything, however bizarre or unachievable it may seem at first. It can be treated as a game if necessary. Drawing up a wish list with a child does not mean it can be granted, but it does mean you will reach some better understanding of where or who or how they would like to be. What if…

This thinking, undertaken with the child and family, should follow a logical pattern, and start with the more usual means of meeting any particular need. Why can't the path that would apply for a non-disabled child be followed? What are the barriers? Are they real, or artificial? Can they be removed? Who needs talking to?

An example might help.

An immediate wish might be identified as *'to play with other children of similar age'*. The options for meeting this could be listed as:

- Hospitalisation where there are lots of other disabled children;
- Special nursery;
- Local playgroup
- Visit friends' homes;
- Invite friends round;
- Join friends in street;
- Take a whole party of children out, say, to the swimming baths.

Stage five: advantages and disadvantages

Stage five is to list the advantages and disadvantages for each of the possible options identified to meet any want. In terms of the example above, the advantages of the more institutional solutions would be plenty of adult supervision, no demands on parents, physical safety. The disadvantages would be that the child was away from home, mixing only with sick and disabled children, unlikely to establish long-term friendships, and at risk of abuse from strangers.

The advantages of the home-based solutions centre on normality, playing at home with familiar toys and establishing more lasting friendships, being able to choose friends and settings and do the kind of things other children, such as siblings, are seen to do. Skills such as sharing and experiences such as quarrelling and making up are more easily developed with a more settled friendship group, and where children have such things as their own toys and their own territory. Disadvantages centre on prejudices of other parents, who resist letting their 'normal' children mix and who may transmit such prejudices to children. Parents may fear lack of supervision, or of children being abducted in the street. There may seem to be too much work involved in clearing up, and transport problems and expense may be issues.

In undertaking such an analysis, it can be seen that many of the disadvantages that emerge from possible plans relate to the parents, not the child. Second, many of the disadvantages are things that can be worked on. In such cases, it is the provision of social work as *a service,* as distinct from the social worker as assessor, which should be noted on the assessment. In the long-term it is only by identifying social work as a means of meeting need and by costing it as part of any service package that it will be available to families.

A long-term ambition might typically be something like 'to be independent, have a nice home and three children'. Such a plan will have to be broken down into its constituent parts, and each worked on systematically, but the process is the same. There are options for independence, and its meaning should be explored. It does not exclude having help with difficult tasks. Independence is about control over lifestyle, not about undertaking things on one's own. Disabled children should not be discouraged from thinking about having normal families and relationships, and it is better to help them find out about the realities, both the joys and the risks involved, than chasing illusions about 'nice houses and three children' that exclude factors like paying rent or having sexual relationships.

Disabled children should be encouraged to join in with the assessment. A large chart of wishes, options and so on can be drawn up and left with the child. This works as well for minor aspirations such as 'I would like to choose my own clothes' to major changes such as 'I would like to go out without my parents', and can help a child to understand that not all things are possible.

The chart may look something like Figure 1, but there are numerous other ways of dealing with it. The trick is to involve the child as much as possible.

Figure 1

Name: *Kellie*

What I want is: *to choose my own clothes*

How can I get it?

(Possibilities)

Way One	Costs	Good Things	Bad Things
Mail order catalogue	1. *cheap clothes* 2. *postage*	*Can do it at home and by myself*	1. *Not as much fun as in the shops* 2. *Take time to arrive*
Way Two			
Go to shops with a volunteer helper	*Pay fares for helper*	1. *Can see and feel real clothes before choosing* 2. *No parents to interfere*	1. *Tiring* 2. *Trying on will be harder than at home*
Way Three			
Go with my parents	*None*	*Easy to arrange*	*They will interfere*

The best way is: *To go to the shops with a helper for some clothes and to use a catalogue for others.*

My Plan is: *To ask the social worker to find a volunteer and to send off for catalogues myself.*

The final stage: negotiation

Once needs, or ambitions, and options for meeting them have been outlined and discussed, the social worker should enter a period of negotiation with the child and family to establish their preferred way forward, whether or not this seems possible at the time. As well, as a preferred option, it is useful to establish whether there is a second choice, which will provide a fallback position should the first option not work out. At this stage the social worker will be conscious, if she remains child centred, of the possibility of having to advocate for the child to its parents.

This may mean some lateral thinking, which could run along the line of: *'Your child would prefer to see her friends here at home, and to have you be there to play with them and to cook tea for everyone. You are concerned by the state of the house, as it takes all your time to care for the child's personal needs, and everywhere is cramped by wheelchairs, rollators and bean bags. You say that there really isn't room to entertain children here, but maybe the real issue is your embarrassment at not having the same facilities as the other parents.'*

Both counselling and advice might help. The embarrassment is self-generated and can be worked upon. Children may enjoy a chaotic environment anyway and sending out for a pizza is fun. It would certainly be cheaper for the social services than funding care for the child in an institutional setting, although it is accepted that not all budgets are yet that flexible!

At the end of the day, it may be that the family and the social worker disagree about the best way forward. There will come a point where they will have to agree to differ, acknowledge that factor and record both points of view in the assessment documentation. While this does not in itself remove the power differential between social worker and parent, it is probably preferable to the more traditional approach in which only the social worker's view is recorded.

...brokerage...

Once preferred options and plans are agreed and established, the social worker may have to undertake a brokerage role. This will depend on the organisation. Some authorities have established assessment teams whose function ends with the recommendations. Brokerage is not particularly new as a task, although the terminology is, and the worker may be in control of a budget. If so, there arise conflicts for the worker of managing the budget on behalf of her employer, and trying to obtain the best deal on behalf of the child. The tasks of managing the authority's budget and advocating for the child are in conflict with each other, and a social worker employed as a care manager cannot reasonably also act as an independent advocate for the child. There may also be problems in acting as a broker with service providers, since the pressure may be to make use of block contractual arrangements, fill places that are funded but empty and seek the cheapest possible option. Social workers may also be under pressure to use the facilities of their own organisation.

The child and family may be protected to some extent by the worker's professional ethics, but the organisational pressures are undeniable, and certainly not confined to social work. Educationalists and medical practitioners managing limited budgets face the same pressures to ration.

The use of independent advocates should be a serious consideration to offset these dilemmas, and help ensure that the child's best interests are not contaminated by organisational pressures. This is not to suppose that advocacy does not have its problems. It may seem to the family that it is yet another worker to get to know and learn to trust.

The brokerage role at its best involves the translation of agreed needs into services that will meet them. The service broker will be equipped with the range of options and agree with the family the course to pursue. She will ascertain what the choices are, if any, and then work out the preferred course, weighing both long- and short-term pros and cons of each, for the child and for the family. The broker will draw up with the family a list of very precise specifications for a service before making a choice: this will be to use an existing service, to adapt one, or to tender for a new provider. The chances are that the social worker turned broker will not have a budget of their own, but will be negotiating with a team manager or applying to a panel or committee for funding. In some cases preventive monies can be diverted and turned over to parents to buy their own services, involving the social worker as a source of advice and experience about the legalities, advantages and pitfalls of directly employing staff or of buying in a service from an agency. This kind of expertise is not yet widespread among social workers, although those used to advising disabled people on the same issues in the days of the Independent Living Fund will have a measure of experience.

Tendering is unlikely to be by an advert in the press, but by sending the agreed service specifications to a range of agencies and asking whether they can provide it and at what cost. Alternatively, it may be that a friend or neighbour can help, usually by getting an agency to employ them on a sessional basis. In this way, both health and police checks can be organised. The contract drawn up between service provider and service user is the safeguard between them, and should be prepared with great care, initially for a short period, and subject to review and revision. The means for undertaking these should be built in at the outset. Contracts are formal agreements and avoid taking things on trust in a situation where there are otherwise enormous power imbalances. Most local authorities are learning the legal aspects of these, but it is also important to make use of the contract to write in the detailed arrangements that make the difference between satisfactory service and discontented service users. The broad outlines of many contracts will soon begin to look much the same, but the more specific detail, and its accuracy in meeting need, will vary with individual children and families. The latter can be part of a contract, or perhaps added as a less formal agreement about ways of working, or what will be provided. This means identifying specifics, such as a service user's dislike of having a radio on all the time, or not wanting to be addressed as 'love'. With institutional care, exactly what is included in the basic fee and what are added on as 'extras' should be made very clear. Often quite basic requirements, such as incontinence pads, are not included in the basic price. These details may seem petty or pernickety and they are certainly time consuming in the first instance, but if they matter to the service user, they matter to the success of the service. The effectiveness of the contract will depend on the accuracy of the assessment.

The experience of many local authorities in the early days of adjusting to a contract culture has been that the private sector is more flexible in responding to spot contracts for individual needs. If local authorities are to respond to this competition they need devolved budgets and decision-making on the provider side, at least to a locality manager. Local area negotiations can then occur between care managers and service providers.

...care management...

Care management involves not simply the assessment and brokerage of services, but their review and maintenance. This aspect is most often neglected in the pressure to get on with the next assessment, but continuity of involvement is an important factor for children and families. In mainstream childcare it is accepted that children will have reviews and that they will be part of them.

Social workers should ensure that families can rely on ongoing help without having to engineer a crisis to ask for it. In these days when everything has its price, this cannot be left to goodwill or good intentions. That is the way to broken promises and skimped service. If social work is needed as a continuing support service to a child or family, it has to be identified in the assessment, agreed with the family, and costed as part of the package.

The next section identifies some of the roles social workers might perform as service providers.

Beyond ABC: social work with disabled children

Many of the skills required to help disabled children are identical whether or not the worker has a purchaser or a provider hat on, and the idea that purchasing is somehow more hard headed and cold blooded will only be true if we let it. Good assessment requires sound childcare skills and the ability to communicate with children and get alongside parents. The need to work in an anti-discriminatory way is no different.

In practice, the range of settings for service provision will be wider than for purchasing, and include an increasing contribution from the voluntary sector. This section will mention a range of social work roles, briefly, as they are all well enough documented elsewhere, if not specifically with *disabled* children in mind.

While advocacy is very much a social work role, this is an uneasy companion of care management, since an advocate for the child cannot also be responsible for rationing the budget for the Authority, directly or indirectly. Clearly, advocates should preferably come from an organisation independent of the one being advocated to. The advocate should ideally not expect to need the future good will of the organisation, nor can an effective advocate expect to have a long shelf life in negotiating with the same organisation. Either they collude with the organisation to maintain goodwill, or they are barred from meetings because they refuse to compromise. A single hard bargain for one child can jeopardise the chances of the next one being favourably dealt with. This highlights the difficulty of operating, as advocacy usually does, on behalf of a series of individuals, achieving change for each child, but leaving the basic deficiencies in the system unchanged.

Counselling has already been suggested as a necessary skill to enable children to come to terms with their own difference and to help enhance their own self-esteem. This is an acknowledgement that they are subjected to a continual bombardment of negative attitudes which suggest they would be better people if they were not disabled. This is likely to take its toll. Disabled youngsters often reach a point where they start to question the reasons for their disability and wonder if they have done something bad to deserve it. This will be compounded if they are subjected to abuse, but it should also be remembered that the risk of abuse is higher if the child has a self-concept of badness,or unimportance or is isolated from other children.

More straightforwardly, disabled children start to wonder why they are not allowed to do the same things as their siblings, attend the same school, or go out to discos at night. Disabled children are right to ask these questions and it would be quite wrong to fob them off with answers which reinforce the discrimination they are facing. The fault is with the school or the organisers of the disco for their exclusion policy. Left to fester, such grievances can develop into behavioural problems.

The Children Act reinforces the importance of counselling in that it replaces the directive of the 1980 childcare Act to offer 'advice, guidance and assistance' with 'advice, guidance and *counselling*' (my emphasis). There does not seem to be much evidence that social services departments are actively responding to this, but it may be worthwhile pointing it out.

Groupwork is an option for tackling many of the above issues when children are old enough. Groupwork can have a variety of functions. It is important to be clear about the reasons for setting up a group: its membership, life span and who will facilitate. Painful issues are often raised in a group setting, and the means of mopping up emotions should be considered in advance. More than one facilitator is always best, not least because it is not uncommon for a group member who becomes distressed to remove themselves and they may need to be followed out. Opportunities for groups of disabled youngsters to get together and explore what being disabled means, in a safe environment where they can talk about their feelings, and gain strength from each other, are invaluable. This kind of group needs disabled adult facilitators to work properly, although I am aware of one successful group of young disabled people, all of whom attended a mainstream school, who simply took it upon themselves to meet and talk, offering a supportive network for schoolchildren who experienced themselves as different from the majority, and who shared similar problems in dealing with this.

At its best such a group enables its members to deal better with the non-disabled world, having taken time out to understand themselves and their part in it. There are recognisable dangers that a peer group based on an oppression can deteriorate into a permanent state of victimhood, which a skilled facilitator ought to be able to guide members out of.

Less formal than establishing groups is the role of facilitating networks. Simply, this means putting people in touch, passing on information and sharing experiences. This can be worldwide thanks to modern technology and linking people by Internet may soon be second nature. As with other marginalised groups, such as deaf people or gays, the chances of someone else like you living next door is remote, unless you live in an institution. Networking helps to bind people over physical distances and reshapes the notion of community beyond those people among whom you actually live.

Individual counselling, groupwork and networking are basic methods of service delivery. As well as having value in themselves they can form a platform from which to move on to thinking and acting in a wider context. There cannot be much fundamental change in the lives of disabled children without fundamental changes in attitude and in legislation. This entails operating at a political level to seek changes in education and in the media to achieve different understandings of childhood, disability and civil rights. To engage in this, social work has to understand its own place in society and to have some sense of direction for itself to support children and parents legitimately by sharing skills, knowledge, understanding and time.

Chapter 6:
Getting Alongside: Working with Parents of Disabled Children

> *The people who make such a fuss about the handicapped's right to life do not realise the burdens parents have to bear. Since Linda's birth I have never been free from anxiety. She is, and will always be, a handicap. She loves me and I love her, but I still wish she had never been born.*
>
> Parent (quoted in Furneaux 1988)

Powerful emotional reactions are inevitable for those who choose to work with disabled children and with their parents. There are strong, polarised viewpoints about the right to life, the needs and responsibilities of parents, the rights of the child, and whether or not it is the property of its parents or an individual in its own right. Social workers might like to reflect on their own reactions to the statement of the parent above. Are you empathising with the parent, or wondering how you would respond as a professional to such a confidence? Do you imagine the parent's burden to be about a lack of physical resources, and resolvable, or concerned with a more intractable emotional need? Are you wondering why as a society we impose such dilemmas on people?

Or are you wondering how the child feels?

Working within an anti-oppressive framework is no less important when dealing with parents or carers than with children directly. The oppressive forces which place disabled children at the bottom of society's pecking order also affect their parents and those who provide education and welfare services for them. Such work is not normally understood within such a framework: the emphasis on medical models of individual pathology is much more prevalent, and the literature is full of articles about the need for mourning for the non-disabled child and on how to help parents adjust to their loss. It cannot be emphasised enough that models based on bereavement are not appropriate when the child is not dead.

Parents may be made to feel inadequate simply by having a child who is not perfect. They may experience guilt, particularly if they have ignored advice to stop smoking, to have an abortion, or to have a child at all 'at their age'. They may transfer the blame on to the child for causing problems for them as parents, thus casting themselves as victims and deserving of sympathy. Like the parent in the quotation above, they may rail more widely against anyone who advocates that a disabled child has the right to life.

Parents may themselves be labelled as 'special' because they are seen as undertaking a parenting task over and above that normally expected. While some parents may enjoy such recognition and even make a career out of it, for most it is a poor substitute for adequate help. Simply labelling parents as 'special' leaves responsibility firmly with them as individuals, rather than acknowledging that societal responsibility for creating and defining a great deal of what constitutes disability should be matched with responsibility for raising and educating disabled children. According some parents the status 'special' is essentially hypocritical and disguises the reality that society as a whole discriminates against and marginalises disabled children. In denying them equality of opportunity it erects artificial barriers and creates problems for them and for their parents.

It is worth noting that disabilism is not the only discriminatory hazard for parents. Parents may encounter a range of pressures relating to their children, their own lifestyle, environment, or attitude of others and it is important not to assume that having a disabled child is always something fundamentally more difficult than parenting other children. There are all kinds of reasons why raising a disabled child in one family in one area might be an easier task for parents or carers than raising a non-disabled child in another. In our intolerant and unequal society, parenthood is made harder for single, disabled or lesbian parents, for those in poverty or from minority racial groups, those living in high rise flats or remote rural areas, those with unsympathetic employers, violent partners, demanding or sick parents or aggressive nextdoor neighbours.

While acknowledging that raising a disabled child is not necessarily harder than raising a non-disabled child, there is an important qualitative difference. Unlike the examples above, the problem becomes centred on the child for being different from other children and as often as not also from its own parents. While this difference should not inevitably result in the child being pathologised, that is what usually occurs in reality. There are enormous cultural pressures to conform as closely as possible to the normality of able-bodied existence, and those disabled children survive best who can achieve the best fit to an able-bodied model.

Just as society expects a disabled child to fight and overcome their disability and become a 'super-crip', it also puts pressure on parents to become 'super parents'. These pressures can result in behaviours which range from reluctance to seek help, since the problem is self inflicted and shameful, to the opposite pole of aggressive, demanding behaviour which seeks both to compensate and to demonstrate 'good parenting' by ensuring that *their* child 'has the best'. It is possible that these pressures either to hide the child or to be demonstrably super parents are greater for members of racial minorities, who are already marginalised by society and have to work that much harder to succeed. Is a disabled child perceived as more of a failure in a community which has its back against the wall?

These contradictory and complex dynamics mean that working with parents requires sensitivity and understanding, and the need to keep constantly in mind that they are ordinary people reacting to abnormal pressures. Both as individuals and as groups, they need support, confidence and a belief in their rights and those of their child to equality as citizens.

It is not always acknowledged that parenting is a skill which has to be learned like any other. Parent craft classes are available to teenage mothers and to parents with learning disabilities, but the majority of parents are supposed to pick it up as they go along or from others such as grandparents. In such ways both good and bad practices are perpetuated. The skills required in raising a disabled child are not different, but they may require some additional learning, and unlearning. To parent a disabled child well its parents have to learn to counter disabilist attitudes: in neighbours, in friends, shops, schools, the health service and perhaps, first and foremost, in themselves. Then they have to learn how to teach their children to do the same. The social work role is not to judge, to preach, or to be a guide to good parenting, but to support and encourage an awareness of the discriminatory world which the disabled child has entered,and which she must negotiate and live in. This means applying anti-discriminatory practice to work with disabled children and their families. This is not easy: nor is there any long tradition of it within social work, which has tended to pathologise the child, work to a paramedical model, and offer little more than sympathy and respite to the family.

I have stated before that working with disabled children and their parents is one of the most difficult areas of social work, yet least regarded by organisations and management (Middleton 1992). This reflects the low value which society places on disabled children and also the enduring myth that the most macho and high-profile tasks in social work are necessarily the most skilful. I am minded to mention this at the outset to warn that almost anything that follows in this chapter could be prefaced with a raft of caveats, and that the reality of actually doing the business with individual children and families will probably never follow any pattern. I hope this initial statement will avoid the necessity to keep repeating it throughout.

If the aim is to get alongside and into a partnership with parents, it is important to start by shedding any assumptions which our own conditioning in a disabilist society may have left us with. Parents should not be pathologised by the social worker any more than the child. Assumptions that it is all bad all of the time need leaving behind until the parents' own reality can be explored. Parents do not necessarily need counselling: they may not need any help at all. They *do* need to know where they can ask for help if things worry them, and not to feel afraid, stigmatised or embarrassed in doing so. The priorities of service deliverers should be clear enough for parents to know what is considered a legitimate request. Given the current discouraging state of much of social services, it may well be that there are many people who need help, but who have been deterred from asking for it. The rest of this chapter assumes that this particular hurdle has been overcome.

It is important, as in any social work relationship, to try and start where the parents are, and not where some other professional's casenotes, or (even worse) some textbook, tells you they should be. In approaching parents of disabled children, the social worker should not lose sight of the underpinning elements of what parenting is all about. It carries both rewards and responsibilities. Children will suffer if their parents do not look after them properly. All children have lots of needs and are hard work. The balance of reward and responsibility may be perceived as skewed where a child is disabled: harder work for less reward. But this does depend very much on what parents expect from the experience and what rewards them as individuals. Only the parents themselves have the answer to this, and they may well not have stopped to consider it.

Given the high probability that the disabled child is a firstborn, the parents may be relating the reality of the child to imagined expectation which is not tempered by any firsthand experience of parenthood at all. Both expectations and realities need to be explored, if only to counter the belief that all the problems of parenting are attributable to the disability and require abnormal solutions. The chances are that the advice of friends and family is still as good (or as bad) as it would have been if the child were not disabled. These explorations can usually be undertaken gently, and with humour, since the aim is to steer the parents back into the paths of normal behaviour, not to sit and preach some arcane expertise relating to disability. Where the disabled child is second or later in the family, this approach serves to reaffirm the parents' own experience as still valid and helps to remove some of the ridiculous and unhelpful mystique which has developed around raising disabled children.

Parents are not passive recipients of welfare, and an understanding of their interpretation of the situation is basic to the social work task. The temptation to rush in and offer the first material thing or service that springs to mind is very strong, but probably ultimately unhelpful, even though this may be what the parents also expect.

It is worth recognising the feeling in ourselves which engenders this common response: parents may be telling a very long story which may be painful and full of problems. Picking this up as a listener can be very distressing and elicit a growing sense of helplessness. Social workers usually take up the job because they want to help people, and the pressure that is felt to do something can be very great. Some parents will actually challenge the worker to act reflecting their experience that there is no help to be had. This happens particularly with a new worker, increasing the vulnerability of the social worker to react too fast in order to gain approval. While listening to a long story, it is possible that at some point an escape route will flit through the social worker's mind: some advice or action which will justify their visit. It is seized upon and offered, without proper assessment; without weighing the options; and as often as not in order to meet the social worker's need to be needed.

Worse, social workers sometimes go to great lengths to persuade parents to take up the service they have suggested only to wonder in days or weeks to come why it was not a success. The trick is to slow down. There really is a great deal of listening to be done before any meaningful help can be offered or any decisions reached about the form which any such help should take.

It is likely that the appropriate response will not involve a specialist disability service at all, since parents' needs are the same whether or not the child is disabled. Such issues as sharing the care, having time to themselves, having a routine and feeling in control are the same for all parents. What may be necessary to explore are the barriers to meeting these needs which may be artificially erected by service providers or informal helpers because of the fact of disability.

The emphasis on listening before offering an 'off-the-shelf' service is not to deny the organisational pressure under which some workers will find themselves to assess, act and exit with as much speed as possible. It is not a position I am prepared to collude with, nor with those social workers who use the pressure from their employer as an excuse to parents for hurried or inadequate work. Such pressure may be real and may need to be tackled on various fronts, but normally it should not be passed on to parents. There is usually scope for reviewing the use made of the time spent with parents. They do not want to waste time either and getting down to business is as good a way of building a relationship as chitchat about the weather. Social work with disabled adults and children has been guilty of being unfocused and unplanned, with workers having no clearer idea of the reason for their visit than keeping in touch. This is for local volunteers and friends. Some casefiles read like novels which track events in a child's life, but do not record any intervention. Social workers are far too expensive to have no idea about what they are doing or why they are doing it.

It is important to acknowledge that listening is a service in itself, and the time given to it is justified even if there is no other service outcome. Having someone who will listen and not make reciprocal demands to be heard can relieve a great deal of stress as well as help people to sort out things in their own mind. It is only when someone falls into a distressed pattern of repeating the same story over and over again that some action may be necessary to assist them to move on.

It is nearly always best if the social worker who first meets the family can continue working with them, avoiding needless repetition by the family and the need to establish trust over and over again. Only where this is impossible because of resource pressures on limited staff is the following method of initial assessment and long-term work as distinct roles acceptable.

Where organisational pressure to prioritise work becomes irresistible it should at least be attempted on a rational basis. It does not necessarily take forever to undertake some initial analysis based on likely outcomes in terms of urgency, importance and the nature of the intervention which might be needed. It does, however, require a worker who is able to analyse and appreciate situations quickly, and who can draw a distinction between urgency and gravity of need. Some situations are very important and serious, but do not necessarily require a response that day. Indeed they may need a long-term strategy. Others are less grave, but do need urgent attention. Clearly there will also be situations which are both important and which require urgent attention., but they are not inevitably the most demanding of resources.

This initial assessment is a skilled task and requires an experienced, clear thinking worker. It is too often left to the vagaries of an unqualified receptionist and conducted in public or over the telephone, with inevitable timewasting later on in the process where workers are despatched with unnecessary haste to some families while neglecting more urgent situations. If competently conducted, an initial assessment should assist in planning and prioritising work and in allocating the right worker. This is a sounder basis on which to proceed than practices more commonly adopted: responding first to those who shout loudest - or by a crude system of prioritisation which assumes that diagnostic categories equate with urgency or degree of need, or on a 'first come, first served' basis, although the latter queuing system is probably the more readily understood by people as equitable.

Initial investment by a skilled worker is required to assess whether, for example:

1. there is an urgent problem and the parents are asking for and in need of immediate help;
2. the parents do not recognise any need for help, but there is concern for the child;
3. there is a problem and the parents are asking for help, counselling and support but on a less urgent basis;
4. parents are asking for help or support, but there is no concern for the child, and there is no current problem identified;
5. no help is required, and there is no concern for the child, but parents are open to continuing contact;
6. parents require no help, there is no concern for the child, and they indicate no wish for any contact.

The nature of the organisation and its own priorities will determine the fate of these or other groups. Clearly some will be closed; some diverted to other organisations; some offered social work help, individually or in groups; some allocated to other workers. In the complaint culture of the 1990s, those who are dissatisfied are much more likely to let us know and it is important to be clear why some are offered help and others not.

There are a standard and practised range of social work interventions including assessment, counselling, casework and child protection, which are well documented if not always necessarily applied to disabled children.

Done adequately, an initial assessment will identify not only the degree of urgency of a situation and its relative importance but may also indicate that many parents may be better helped through groupwork, rather than on an individual basis. This carries the additional advantage of increasing the possibilities for collective action. The following is a suggested framework for an assessment of parents' needs. I have avoided the use of the term 'carer's assessment' for two reasons. First it implies that raising a disabled child is outside the normality of parenthood. Second, most parents do not identify themselves as 'carers'.

This self-identity may be about to change. The Carers (Recognition and Services) Act 1995 comes into force in April 1996. Section 1 (2) identifies carers for disabled children as a group who may request the local authority to assess their 'ability to provide and to continue to provide care'. Since Section 1 (3) of the Act excludes paid carers and volunteers with voluntary organisations from making such requests, the majority of those covered by this section will be parents. In singling out parents of *disabled* children in this way the framers of the legislation are reinforcing the difference between this and the parenting of non-disabled children.

Toward a model of assessment

In constructing a model of assessment for working with parents, it is important not to lose sight of some of the broad themes around assessment in general. The situation, not the individual, is the rightful subject of assessment. It is still important to match services, including social work itself, to need and not vice versa, and it remains vital to regard assessment as an analytical process, not as a system for data collection. The criteria for judging a good assessment are, first, how well the process aids understanding and second, the extent to which problems have been tackled and ambitions realised. The quantity of information collected should not feature as a consideration. I mention this only because so many workers seem to take some pride in how much they have managed to get people to reveal to them and so many organisations seem to find some bizarre intrinsic merit in collecting standardised data. This is the downside of information technology.

In the assessment of the child's situation, the parents are a central ingredient. Similarly, the child is a vital ingredient in a parents' assessment. However, for the social worker, there is now a crucial difference. Despite the fact that the assessment has become centred on adult needs, the interests of the child must still be the primary consideration. This is morally right, and it is the law. It is far too facile and a serious negation of responsibility to adopt the stance I have often encountered that if the parents are OK, then the child is sure to be. While it is probably true in reverse to assert that if the parents are not coping, it is bad news for the child, it does not necessarily follow that the wellbeing of the parents automatically ensures the wellbeing of their child. Indeed, it seems to me a concept promulgated by people who are afraid to face the difficulties involved in considering and consulting the child.

Assessment can be a loaded term. In practice it is too often bureaucratic and insensitive and carried out as an inflexible process done to rather than *with* people. In such cases control is not with the parents, nor even with the worker, but in the distant hands of a person or persons unknown who once compiled the forms. This kind of inequality is disempowering and poor practice. Social workers need to make clear to parents that assessment is related to their situation and is not an assessment of them against some gold standard ideal parent. Such factors as age and experience of parenthood and skills remain relevant but they only matter in context. Social workers are not there to judge people but to engage in making judgements. The difference is crucial.

Second, parents should be clear that the assessment is related to how they see the situation, and they should understand the reason for any information requested. Silly explanations like 'It's on the form' or 'We have to ask everybody that' deserve rude answers. The assessment is a mutual attempt to define, describe, understand and explore.

In summary, assessment will seek to ascertain parental wishes and aspirations for themselves and for the child, establish the barriers to achieving them, review the options for change, weigh them against each other, acknowledge risks and select a way forward.

Collecting information and engaging in discussions in the following areas may be helpful in achieving these goals. This is not a blueprint, but a series of suggestions which are offered in no particular order of importance.

1. Resources

This should be seen in terms of both practical and personal resources. Practical resources include the financial circumstances of the family. Social workers sometimes have a tendency to avoid dealing with finance, particularly if a welfare rights service exists in the area. Disability benefits are complex and boring but financial help is often also one of the easiest and most practical ways to help. Other practical resources include the type of housing, the location of playgroups, schools, voluntary agencies and so on. Clearly it also includes the presence or absence of family, friends and helpful neighbours.

Personal resources are less tangible. The social worker will need to find out something about the personality of the parents: their skills; mental and physical health; outlook on life; intelligence; spiritual or religious beliefs; and how much grit they have. None of these issues should be approached with a right or wrong answer in the social worker's head, nor should they alone make the judgements. Social workers may need to assess a parent's health, for example, but they may not be the best person to make the judgement. Most people will assess themselves if given the openings. The only broad generalisations I risk are the observations that women tend to judge their personal abilities more critically than men and that younger parents are less realistic than older ones.

2. Coping strategies

If the disability is not subject to cure it has to be integrated into the equation and the situation actively managed. Active management simply means taking control of events and is more helpful than a fatalistic 'wait and see' philosophy. In the long-term it encourages a belief in children that nothing is written in the stars, and that they have the opportunity to make choices and influence their own futures. This is a rare attitude among parents for too many disabled youngsters. Families who wait inactively for a miracle cure are the least helpful in securing a future for their child in which she can actively participate.

Before attempting to plan on this active basis with a family, the social worker will be well advised to try to find out how the family usually deal with things. What do they actually do to manage their lives day to day and to cope with changes? Is this the sort of family that sits down and discusses things, or do they always follow someone's lead? Do they plan ahead, or take each day at a time? How do the individuals in the family normally deal with stress? Do they address problems or hide from them? Do they drink? Disappear out to work? Meditate? How do they look after themselves as individuals or as a group? Do the parents spend time with each other? How do they self-indulge? Is it healthy, like soaking in the bath, or unhealthy, like smoking? What outside interests do they have?

Are they philosophical about life? Do they hold any religious beliefs, or are they without any such framework of understanding?

In drawing up this picture, the social worker should include the contribution of the disabled child and rigorously avoid any temptation to include them simply as a problem. Is the disabled child seen as a member of the family, or as some kind of problematic outsider?

If the family have difficulties in coping it is as likely that these derive from another source, such as housing or finance, as from the presence of a disabled daughter or son.

Most importantly, do the family's usual ways of understanding life and coping with it meet the needs of their disabled member? If so it would clearly be a mistake to disturb them by imposing formula solutions from outside simply because they are more familiar to the social worker or convenient for the social services. It is better to find ways to support the family in maintaining its normal healthy patterns of functioning and as far as possible tailor any additional support to that end.

If the needs of the disabled child cannot be met within the family's normal pattern of operation, more fundamental help is needed if the child is to be supported and protected. This help may not be welcomed since the family may expect the child to change and perseverance, time and care will be required. The assessed need may be for counselling, but will have to be preceded by an acceptance by the family that they are not able to cope with the disabled child without changing themselves. Reaching this realisation may be a painful process as it casts doubt on the success of the parents with non-disabled children in the family. It will be made even more difficult by the fact that one parent will almost certainly reach that kind of understanding ahead of the other. For the child's sake, the social worker needs to reinforce the fact that it is not the child that is the problem but the family's adjustment to the fact of disability.

Gaps in normal coping mechanisms should be identified. For example, if the mother's usual means of coping is to talk about things with a friend, and children constrain her mobility, the gap may be the absence of a phone, or of a sitter, or of access to transport. These may all boil down to financial constraints.

One parent's means of coping may not be helpful for the other. For example if one 'copes' by staying at work for all the hours God sends, then the other cannot get out at all. Parents or partners may need to find time to be with each other. Both also need time to *enjoy* being with their baby so that the reward side of the equation is encouraged. Finding ways to create these quality times is vital.

Uncovering gaps in coping mechanisms may mean talking to each parent individually, as well as together. Fathers in particular are often excluded or exclude themselves, from discussions about disabled children. In some cases the social worker will be the vehicle through which parents share their fears and their feelings. Parents who hide feelings may do so for protective reasons but it is usually unhelpful in the long-term and creates a framework of misunderstanding and mistrust. Assessment as a process will inevitably be slowed by the release of feelings but the appraisal may be all the more accurate. Social workers must resist pressure from new managerialism to break down their work into exclusive stand-alone categories such as assessment and counselling. Many encounters with real people will involve engaging in both activities to facilitate each other. It is important that the social worker be clear as to which activity she is engaged in at any point and she should keep a clarity in her own mind and casenotes about assessment and counselling. She should be alert to the possibility, however, that both occur as overlapping activities during any professional meeting. This is preferable to dividing social work artificially into functions and assuming they will be as effective in helping people.

A good social worker will want to understand how the parents are experiencing their situation. This goes beyond pure description and collection of facts. One method is to ask the parent to describe their own child. Each parent will probably do it differently, as would the child herself, and neither may match the social worker's impression. Some will give a description focusing on the disability because they have been conditioned to that by overexposure to medics and paramedics. They may need encouraging to go beyond that to talk about the child as a person and as a personality. If they cannot, it may indicate real problems but I have found most parents both enjoy and welcome the difference.

Reaching some understanding of how parents view things will enable more appropriate help to be offered by lowering the risk of a mismatch between families' needs and services offered. Social workers in too much of a hurry or who operate only on facts, commonly offer a service that they think, logically, is helpful but which parents may see as pressure or as criticism. The risks of this misunderstanding seem to me to be greater where there are class or racial differences between worker and parents.

As well as reaching an understanding of how the parents interpret their situation and how they feel about it, it is important to explore how they adapt to change. Their understanding of their lives and that of their child will have altered radically and fast with a diagnosis of a disabling condition. Diagnosis, as opposed to suspicion that something is wrong, is usually experienced as a crisis and is reinforced as such by the medical profession, but it is not necessarily a negative experience. Indeed having a label is experienced by some parents as a relief and as justifying their anxieties and concerns about their child.

In my experience, parents who are told about their child's disability can nearly always remember how and by whom and how well they were told, but rarely anything about what they were told. They make little or no sense of it because it is outside their reality. I have always advised parents whose children are being assessed (medically or educationally) to write down the things they wanted to know and take notes as the doctor or official spoke,...even if that meant getting less done in any one consultation. While it is helpful if the social worker is present when parents are told about their child's condition, in practice it is much more likely that the social worker will be dealing with it retrospectively, and as such be responding to the impressions, reactions and emotions as much as to the facts. This can occur years after the event.

Adjusting to the unknown, and sometimes unknowable, aspects of disability can lead to a reliance on experts. Doctors especially are accorded expertise they do not have, as are social workers. It is seductive to take on the mantle but workers should beware of confusing their experience of managing disability in the outside world or within a family, which may help, with an expertise on the particular child which they do not have. The expert on the child is first the parent, and later the child herself although they may not wish to believe it!!! Still less should any worker try to deduce much from the diagnosis. It tells only broad information about a disabling condition, less about the child herself, and nothing at all about the way the family will react. Nonetheless social workers should still trouble to learn the differences between disabling conditions. Both parent and child will expect a measure of knowledge, but they should not confuse the social worker with a healthcare professional.

The parents have to adapt their existing reality to incorporate the new information. This is a dynamic process and in practice many will adapt the fact of disability to fit their existing reality. For example, if disability is seen as a punishment for sins, a child born with a disability may be a matter for shame, even where there is nothing obvious to be ashamed of. Lives may be re-examined and people with such beliefs may question not just 'why me?' but 'what have I done to deserve this?'

If good health is seen as the triumph of mind over matter and disability represents weakness of personality, the necessary adjustment will involve learning that some things cannot be overcome simply by willing it so! Families who are used to being in control over their lives, usually richer ones, often experience great difficulty in adapting to a situation which they cannot buy or bully their way out of.

The same diagnosis to another family will simply confirm their view that they have no control over their lives: the latter family may adapt more easily.

Diagnosis of disability can make parents view the child differently. Again this relates to the value and expectation placed on the child before diagnosis. An only child in a family may carry more of the parental hopes and dreams than one of six, and experience more pressure to achieve.

Some parents describe a diagnosis of disability as like having a different child although of course they have not. Concepts of bereavement and loss counselling have been suggested as models for helping, but I do not think they are appropriate. We need to develop models which relate to the actual situation, not adapt those which relate to death. The child is not dead, nor to be grieved for, nor replaced with a healthy one. The prescriptive nature of much of the work on loss and bereavement is less than helpful even where a child has died, and certainly inappropriate where they have not.

3. Sources of stress

Stress can be created in many different ways, and the following checklist represents a logical breakdown for consideration. It is not suggested that a social worker should sit down with a parent and run through the list, but rather that the areas should be borne in mind and explored as possibilities. Financial problems have already been mentioned. Caring costs money and poor families are bound to suffer extra financial worries if the child is dependent. However, any family can have financial concerns that are unrelated to the disabled child but which are high on their stress list. Assumptions about presence or absence of financial worries should not be made, however poor or rich a family may appear to be. Middle-class parents may be more reluctant to admit to being in financial straits, while disability benefits may be an important part of the family income for poor families.

Emotional stress can be caused by helplessness at watching a child struggle, suffer pain, or die. This is as obvious as it is often ignored. Many adults tend not to demonstrate feelings. We hesitate to be tender, we swallow anger and frustration and we cry on our own. Identifying, legitimating and releasing such feelings can constitute part of an assessment as well as starting the healing process. Sharing such feelings with a professional worker in confidence is often a helpful step. No reciprocation is required and there are no embarrassing aftermaths at social gatherings.

Sheer tiredness is also a cause of stress as well as creating a dangerous situation for parents and children. Lack of sleep is a commonly reported feature of parents of disabled children, as are fights about feeding, the wear and tear of hospital visits, the need to plod to a different school which may be some distance away and deal with a different set of officials, as well as having to receive a stream of therapists at home. It all adds up.

Some of these stresses feed themselves. For example anxiety about a child not sleeping can be a self-fulfilling prophecy. The child picks up parental lack of routine or overanxiety in settling them down and stays awake. The parent fails to sleep, becomes more anxious, loses even more routine and consequently gets even more tired. Ironically, this vicious circle seems to affect those parents who are at home with time and space to develop anxiety patterns more than it does working parents who have neither time nor energy to do anything in the evening but go to sleep. Their child is more likely to oblige by doing the same.

The family itself may constitute a source of stress: most do after all! The main burden for a parent may not be the disabled child. It could be another child, a parent, or the partner. One in two marriages now end in divorce without any assistance from disabled children. That a disabled child is an easy scapegoat for a family's ills does not mean they are the cause of them.

Social causes of stress are often present. The inadequacies of public transport or the sheer effort of moving a disabled child and all her paraphernalia may trap parents in their homes. Holidays are more complicated. In some cases, neighbours are ignorant, cruel and sometimes downright hostile. Friends sometimes drift away. Communities can reject as well as support. Single parents, lesbian mothers, members of racial minorities, those in poverty or poor housing or those who live a long way from extended families may be under additional stresses not related to the child.

Additional stress can be caused by the very things intended to help. Poor information about service provision and poor provision itself add to problems. Services that are inflexible, unreliable, not individually geared, ethnically insensitive, costly and stigmatising can increase rather than ease stress, especially where a family feels it has no choice in the situation. The school or education department may be a site for conflict rather than a source of support.

4. Support

In making an assessment, actual and potential sources of support have to be identified as well as problems and sources of difficulty and stress. The latter can be related to the former. Indirect help can also be identified, such as child minding for the non-disabled child. Support can be organised through networks, voluntary groups, churches. Circles of support can be set up involving small groups of parents and friends who undertake to watch out for each other. It is important to consider using ordinary facilities, and not to assume that a disabled child means that something special is required.

Support is sometimes available, but impossible or impractical to access, or there may be reasons why parents do not want to make use of it. On a practical level this may be because potential helpers are too far away, child minding is too expensive or parents' groups are geared up for the needs of white or middle-class people.

On an emotional level parents can throw up barriers which may be addressable by sensitive counselling. A disabled child is often regarded by parents as their problem, or even punishment and their sole responsibility. Guilt or shame is dealt with by refusing help and a stubborn persistence in handling the matter within the family. Where the father feels the shame and the mother does the bulk of the handling, the problem is compounded. It is unfortunate that many men still regard the birth of a disabled child as some reflection on their manhood. This is compounded by the attitude of friends and colleagues who are likely to share the same philosophy. I have found the worst instances of this in Army families where the attitudes of senior officers compounded the problem, indicating this to be less an issue of class and more one of gender. Such men may deny the existence of problems and deprive both mother and child of help or understanding. In some cases they can deny the existence of disability at all: Janice Pink notes her own father's reaction to her inability to learn to ride a bicycle: '*...There was nothing wrong with his offspring. How dare they? The very thought!*' (Pink 1994).

Parents may be embarrassed either by their child per se or by some aspect of their difference or behaviour. Incontinence, feeding problems, fits or unusual behaviour may prove easier to hide away than to explain.

Another barrier to accepting help lies in the inability to reciprocate. Many people dislike taking something for nothing and the impossibility of returning the help offered, say to babysit, can be a powerful disincentive. This attitude may be based on an untested assumption that there is no satisfaction for the babysitter in looking after a disabled child. There may be undiscovered ways of returning favours.

More serious is a distrust of the motivations of others which may sometimes have a genuine basis. Disabled children are vulnerable to abuse and inevitably potential abusers find it convenient to take jobs which bring them into contact with easy targets. False reassurance is unreasonable in such circumstances: helpers need to be carefully checked out either officially or through talking with other service users. Odd behaviour on the part of the helper or evident distress on behalf of the child should never be ignored.

This does not mean that the majority of people who seek to help are not perfectly genuine. Some people get satisfaction out of helping although others find such a thing deeply mystifying. There is nothing wrong with getting satisfaction out of helping others, provided the child being helped benefits from the experience.

The fear of criticism of their childcare skills rides high with many parents and is a barrier to sharing the care of their children with others. Children often behave better for carers other than their parents. They usually know they can play-up their parents without losing their love. However, this better behaviour can sometimes result in the temporary carers being perceived, or perceiving themselves, as the more skilful and criticising the natural parents.

A variation on this is simply differences of opinion about how to raise a child. Grandparents can be accused of spoiling the child and disrupting painstaking therapeutic programmes. These barriers often mask deeper fears. Grandparents are supposed to spoil children after all.

Not wanting to be identified as a problem family can be a barrier. This may manifest itself in a general antagonism to social services which is widely regarded as a service for families who cannot cope without good cause or who abuse their children. Avoiding seeking help may simply be a wish to maintain normal social patterns and not appear to be different. While these are both potentially problematic as barriers to help, they are healthy starting-points from the perspective of the child. Finding ways to manage that are as near to the family's normal social pattern as possible and using ordinary valued facilities which non-disabled people use are a good basis for ensuring that the child is less likely to be scapegoated or blamed for spoiling everyone else's lifestyle.

5. Areas of conflict with child's interests

So far the areas for assessment have been relatively unproblematic although sophisticated counselling skills are required as follow up to some of the above. It may prove more difficult to explore areas where the child's needs are in conflict with those of the parents, particularly if it is the social worker rather than the parent who identifies possible conflict. It is helpful to explore these with parents in an open and supportive manner, and to acknowledge that many such conflicts are normal. This is far more effective than simply making a mental note at the time, recording the matter later in the casefile and thus avoiding dealing with the issue until a later occasion. In the first place it is unethical. In the second, it is likely to be less accurate than if the parents identify areas of conflict themselves. In the third place, there is far less chance of being able to work with the parent to find a solution if trust has been abused by the social worker in such a way. This rule applies even in cases of possible abuse: most parents do not want to abuse their children, and will be more inclined to be helped if any concerns are shared with them.

Conflicts of interest can arise in various ways. One example would be a parent's wish for her child to attend a special needs playgroup in order to meet other parents, but which deprives the child of a range of experiences and may even preprogramme her for special schooling. Another would be when the parent refuses to have a helper in her home because she regards it as an intrusion, and so sends the child to institutional respite instead.

Some women seem to need a 'baby' and a disabled child can provide a long-term source of such comfort, but at the cost of denying the disabled child the chance to grow. Maintaining dependence in a disabled child is tolerated in a way in which it would not be if the child were able-bodied since such mothers are accorded sympathy and their needs allowed to override those of the child. In all these examples the social worker has to find a way to meet the underlying need of the parent in a different way so that the child's interests are not damaged.

In identifying and managing areas of conflict between parent and child it is helpful to acknowledge the particular pressures on the mother to be the principal carer within a patriarchal system. Mothers are normally expected to take the time to care for the child at home, take her to hospital, meet the school teachers and engage with the social services. This expectation is at the expense of their own lives, needs and aspirations much more than for fathers. Mothers who are themselves oppressed and undervalued may place unrealistic expectations on their children to fill the emotional gaps in their lives. The child's failure to meet the mother's needs may lead to abuse or neglect, either directly or by the mother ignoring the abuse by the father. The blame for the mother's unhappiness is directed at the less powerful child rather than at the powerful father. It is important that social workers challenge, rather than reinforce, the stereotypes of marriage and motherhood which are at the root of these dynamics. This means not placing pressure on women to 'cope' as a matter of principle, but acknowledging their difficulties as legitimate and seeking ways to support them. The social work role is not simply to investigate or monitor to identify and protect the child at risk, but to offer support to women to reduce the pressure on them. In this way, the dangers of conflict of interest between mother and child are reduced.

In saying this, it is also necessary to acknowledge that many of the pressures which threaten women's mental and physical health are structural and relate to broad issues such as poverty, poor housing, racism, unemployment and crime. These have to be challenged politically through collective action, but while we wait for the cultural wheels to turn in a more favourable direction, it matters that we do not fall into the trap of blaming the victims.

6. Personal ambitions/expectations

Given that the assessment is about the parents' circumstances, it can be helpful to explore their expectations and views of what parenting is all about for them. In this, talking about their own experiences of being parented can be useful. Beyond this the parents will have other personal goals and ambitions. The fact of a disabled child may have altered the parents' own life plans and the change may be welcome or it may not. Thwarted ambition may be retrievable or it may not. If the adjustments that have been made are resented, the social worker should be exploring ways to find time to replace, adjust or revisit these.

It may be relevant to know whether or not the child was planned, and if not whether the pregnancy was welcomed or resented.

7. Siblings

To complete a picture of the family, the role undertaken by the siblings is vital, as well as their perceptions about what is problematic and what is good. Are their own concerns trivialised in the face of the much greater perceived difficulties of their disabled sister or brother? Are they expected to act more reasonably and more maturely than their friends? Are they teased at school or in the street? Do they feel the need to keep the fact of their disabled sibling a secret? Are they consulted about family plans? Are they angry at the lack of attention they get? The chances are high that siblings will be fond of their disabled brother or sister and that they will take a caring role. Any assessment should be as mindful of their needs as of the more obvious ones of the disabled child. It is important not to stereotype either as problem child and angelic

Young Carer, or as poor unfortunate and 'Don't know how lucky you are!'. Reality is rarely so straightforward.

The aim of the assessment process is to identify ways to help parents actively to manage their situation: to seek a working partnership. The final step, having collected and discussed all the relevant information, is to work out with the parents a plan either for the next few days or over a year or more. Whether it is short or longer term the plan should be subject to review as circumstances change, or if it does not seem to be working. Rather than providing a blueprint, its function is to give some sense of direction and control. It follows that it is not appropriate when reviewing the plan to assess success or failure, but its continued relevance, or otherwise, in terms of the goals that were set.

Dealing with oppression

Undoubtedly it would be easier to avoid this issue or to couch it in less challenging language, but that would be to ignore the reality of growing up in this society for thousands of children. Adults who become disabled in later life may have to face their own disabilist attitudes and deal with changes in values for themselves and for their supporters. In the process many become very angry with the rest of the world which is still able-bodied. The adoption of the terms 'disabled' and 'temporarily able-bodied' for the two sectors of society reflect this anger, as well as seeking to remind the majority that their non-disabled condition may change at any time.

A similar change of attitude may be required of parents who have not previously thought about the implications of having a disabled child, or who have only regarded their situation as some kind of horror that affects other people. If the parents do not address issues of disabilism it is ultimately unhelpful for the child, who may grow up in the belief that the disability is her own problem to overcome and with a continuing need to prove something.

It is not, of course, going to help for a social worker to charge into a family who see the child as a victim of an impairment and themselves as struggling to do their best for her, to tell them that they are part of the oppressive process which denies disabled children a full and equal place in society. There are more appropriate approaches to consider.

Demonstrating different attitudes and approaches is almost always going to be more effective than engaging in theoretical argument. Neither should it be assumed that dealing with the issue directly is the most effective: parents may take more notice of other parents, or of disabled adults who have personal experience of managing oppression.

If the social worker is lucky, there may be influential parents in the area who hold the view that disabled children are the victims of discrimination. Parents who are disabled themselves can be extraordinarily influential if they adopt such beliefs, but not all disabled adults are in tune with a social model of disability. Social workers wishing to make some of their own luck can improve the odds if they know a lot of families. Working with or from centres undoubtedly helps here. Backing up these parents in group discussion, in their approach to organisations and in their dealing with their children's situations can help influence others both by role modelling and through exchanges of views. The social work role becomes facilitative in putting people in touch with each other. There is, of course, an organisational responsibility for such information, which should not depend on individual social workers building personal contacts, but in practice the embryonic state of services for disabled children will make this unrealistic in most authorities. The most practical step at the moment is for social workers to establish networks to exchange ideas and information.

Many parents may not have any exposure to viewpoints other than the medical model. This does not mean they will be unreceptive to hearing them, nor of changing approaches when they can be demonstrated to make sense. Change, unlike charity, may not be best starting in the more personally threatening home environment, but in the family's dealing with outside agencies. Many parents find the move from the question to a school of 'How is my child doing?' to the more pertinent 'What is the school doing for my child?' an empowering one. In making it they are moving away from pathologising the child to challenging the education authority to do its job. While the process of ensuring the latter may be just as long and draining, the conceptual shift away from blaming the child is helpful and lasting, and will translate into other areas of life. It may be necessary to help parents manage the reality of how best to challenge as well as shifting concepts. Aggressive fighting talk is rarely as helpful in the long-term as taking an assertive stance. Sharing some experience on how to approach agencies and organisations can be empowering.

Once adopted as a philosophy it can underpin the parents' dealings on behalf of the child. The move away from apologising because their child is different towards challenging service providers of all kinds is positive. The list is endless. The library should be asked to recommend, seek out and supply books for children which show disability, and disabled children, in a positive light. Cafés should be asked for a table which is accessible for a wheelchair, and to provide a menu in large print. In beginning to challenge, rather than apologise, parents will need to develop a thick skin, but they will also stop feeling ashamed of their child, or needing to hide her away. This is good for the child, who will learn perhaps that many people are thoughtless, but that the need to change is theirs, not hers. Both parents and children should develop confidence in their own expertise about the child, about her needs, limitations and aspirations, and where the real barriers lie. Sorting out which barriers result from the impairment and which from the way the world deals with it is crucial.

In the section on social work practice, I suggested that social workers ask the question of themselves *'Would I consider that option if the child were not disabled?'*. If the answer is 'no', the social worker should be able to give good reasons for the difference. This helps to sort out whether the service is based on sound childcare principles and whether a lower standard is being accepted. A similar approach can be taken with parents, who are as conditioned as anyone else to believe that something different has to be done where a child is disabled. Applying different standards without sound reasons has resulted in such tragedies as teenagers with learning disabilities sexually abusing children because no one had thought it necessary to offer them any sex education, nor corrected them when they exposed themselves or masturbated in public. A child being spoonfed when sitting on his mother's knee is one thing: a young man of seventeen doing the same thing causes raised eyebrows. Treating a growing disabled child differently from others of his age group when such difference is not justified serves only to reinforce abnormality and separate him from his peers. Down's syndrome children who are educated separately from other children may seem to be protected, but are disadvantaged in their learning opportunities by reduced chances to hear and imitate normal speech.

Working with parents entails not just problem solving, but counselling with a view to exploring attitudes and values, their child's place in the world, and barriers to understanding. This may mean exploring and freeing their bad feelings, disappointments, anger and frustrations and legitimating them, before helping people to move on. Such feelings are normal enough, but have to be dealt with and directed appropriately if the parents are to work for the benefit of their child. Parents have responsibility for another life: that of their child. In accepting that, some understanding of the threats to their child's wellbeing has to be reached, and with it an understanding of the discrimination she is inevitably going to face as a child and as an adult with a disability.

In reaching this, parents will discover they are less alone with the challenge of raising a disabled child than they may have thought at one time. The problem is much bigger than themselves and their child, and the solution, necessarily, is also much bigger. Change at personal and family level is key to the process, but change is also required at community and societal level. While it does seem incredibly slow compared with the speed at which a child grows up, change is happening, and it happens because people continue to refuse to accept that things are good enough.

Nonetheless, it follows that parents who operate in groups or through organisations are more likely to be effective in improving conditions for disabled children than those who battle alone for their own child. Organisations much prefer the latter: if they look like having a good case they can be picked off individually and the affair quietly settled 'out of court' without setting any awkward precedents. While it is hard to blame parents who adopt such strategies, they are short-lived gains, and only benefit one child. Directing parents to groups concerned with improving the rights of disabled children is ultimately going to be more effective. If none exist, it would be a legitimate use of time to help some parents to start one.

Oppression on an individual level, for the child, also has to be addressed. If the parent is not ready when their child gets picked on, this will be all the harder. Parents may benefit from some discussion, either with the social worker or with other parents, about managing the child's feelings of difference, her attitude toward her own body, and dealing with others. If parents are able-bodied, as is the case with most parents of disabled children, they will have no personal experience to draw on of how it feels to be disabled, nor of how to manage the behaviour of others. I do not think they should worry unduly about this: some disabled adults also have a very poor idea of how to manage discrimination, and may make more enemies than allies in trying to address it. Everyone, if they are honest, will know that society is on a steep learning curve in this area, and that it is trying to find balances between such things as helping and patronising; gratitude and ingratiation, pride and arrogance; independence and isolation.

As much as anyone, able-bodied parents have a legitimate role in helping to dismantle oppression. Indeed, as parents of children who are discriminated against, and regarded as second class, they may themselves experience marginalisation from the world of parents whose children are 'normal'. This may involve actual physical separation, such as the mother being moved to a side ward in the maternity hospital, or the more lasting but less tangible feeling that people are treating them differently. The tendency of some parents to compare their children's progress on a competitive basis with others can hurt where the standards for comparison are set in a physical or intellectual context.

Children are not born with discriminatory attitudes about race, sexuality or disability. Before they learn such attitudes they are likely only to be curious.

Listening to children talking with each other about their disability is usually salutary and can be funny. These are the halcyon days! Hangups develop later when some children learn to be cruel and others to mind about it. Disabled children learn to be prickly about answering questions, accepting help or being self-conscious about different eating or drinking patterns.

At these times parental help and support is needed to reassure the disabled child that the other child is in the wrong, and that she has as much right to be in the world as they do. It is not easy, because at much the same time, the disabled child is not only realising that she is different, but also that she is in a less valued minority group. Adults in oppressed minority groups usually seek support and understanding from others of their kind. This seems to me to be no less important as an option for children, and should strengthen, not diminish, their confidence in relating to non-disabled children.

Conclusion

Parents of disabled children have a very real fight on their hands. As a society we are in the middle of a conservative backlash against the welfare state, with an ideological framework of every man for himself, women and children later. Disabled people are engaged in a fight as a minority to have their civil rights respected and to take an equal place as citizens. There is a legislative framework to equalise rights for women and for black people, and there have been successes in effecting change. Nevertheless, the real power still remains firmly in the hands of the increasingly rich, white establishment, and the prevailing ethos is still to grab as much as you can get, with a punitive approach to those who fail to conform. Vocationalism is replacing professionalism in social work.

In such a climate it is scarcely surprising if parents of disadvantaged children feel a sense of hopelessness, or avoid the whole tacky mess by believing that the child is the problem and focusing attention on curing the child rather than changing the world. Empowerment is not a quick fix answer to all this, but it does offer a framework of hope and possibility within which to work for change in partnership with parents. This means finding ways for disadvantaged people to work together by establishing commonalities, rather than concentrating on or highlighting the differences and issues that divide. As a collective methodology, it can mean groups of parents effecting local change, networking with others on a wider perspective, and even challenging the ways that society thinks. Celebrating and publicising successes, however small each may seem, is more important than dwelling on difficulties.

Postscript:
Social Work Today

The 1990s have seen the increasing dominance of a right-wing, market-orientated culture, that is increasingly hostile to traditional notions of welfare, promotes the pursuit of self-interest as a virtue and accepts the survival of the fittest as a justifiable framework. It is a society based on power which is without moral credibility and without any sense of its own worth. We have experienced years of disintegrating yet arrogant political leadership with an increasingly boring succession of financial and sexual scandals, with subsequent ministerial resignations. Any moral leadership that might have been expected from the Church of England has vanished with its increasingly public display as a white, sexist, homophobic and directionless organisation. As such the Church represents the entrenched establishment at its worst, and at its most dangerous. Sadly, other major religions can be equally narrow minded and all too often become the focal points for intolerance and bigotry.

There are increasing divisions in society not simply between rich and poor, but among the disadvantaged. Not only is the Establishment in disarray, but there is no coherent opposition. The growth of right-wing power has not seen a union of oppressed minorities, but an increasingly divided society, where groups have concentrated more on publicising their own oppression than on seeking co-operative ways to end it for all. Some individuals and small groups have made themselves very important and powerful within limited horizons. Those who do not fit their definitions are excluded from the right to speak, have an opinion or engage in research. Within a divided society it is easier for little fish to think big and become creatures to be reckoned with inside their tiny ponds. The real masters are still in place and have felt increasingly untouchable. The arrogance of the Conservative government has been evidence of this, and moves by the opposition to gain power by emulating it are not encouraging.

There is some evidence that this dismal scenario is changing.

Management by objectives is being replaced in the real business world by an emphasis on people, and we might dare to hope that the wheels of fashion will turn again from social work by competency, the current vogue, to social work as a reflective and responsible professional activity. Everyone has a role to play in dismantling oppression and in working towards a society based on mutual respect for one another in which diversity is encouraged. People from various groups are reaching out to each other in a recognition that it is more important to build on commonalities of experience and possibilities for change than to emphasise difference as a dividing force.

There is clearly a long way to go, but the overt hostility and mocking of the Establishment can be seen as evidence not of failure, but of the effectiveness of disadvantaged groups in gaining a voice. Social work does not have any exclusivity of role either as a keeper of the flame of anti-oppressive practice or in leading the way to a better world. However, it does have a key role in that social workers work with the most disadvantaged and least regarded sections of society. In a society where value and personal worth are based on the exercise of power and the ability to make money, a child is regarded more as a chattel than an individual with rights, and their worth measured by achievement. A disabled child is typically regarded as having little potential and consequently low value.

The focus of change is to emphasise civil rights rather than individual pathology. Disabled children will never achieve recognition as future citizens, let alone equality, while the problems they encounter are seen as rooted within them and their disability, rather than in the disabling, oppressive forces ingrained in the fabric of our society. It is a question of changing the way we think.

As a society we are conditioned to accept a reality packaged for us through television, newspapers and on supermarket shelves. Within a seductive guise of providing us with information, we are conned by marketing people into purchasing largely empty but elegant cardboard or plastic boxes which tell us in picturesque detail all the things they do not contain: no sugar, no preservative, no added water, no monosodium-glutamate. We purchase purity, good health and a sense of wellbeing. If not, we succumb like so many lemmings to just the reverse and childishly rebel against Official Advice, as the manufacturers know we will, and buy expensive packages of leaf and paper that are quite clearly labelled as containing a substance which will kill us or maim our unborn children. This all amounts to bizarre behaviour no visiting Martian could hope to understand.

Neither science nor logic seem to be saving us from illusion. While even young children may know now that the earth is not flat and will correct an adult with alacrity for remarking that the sun is moving across the sky, they are quite likely to believe that there are creatures from outer space who speak American, that warfare is exciting and that the 'dead ' can be re-booted for as long as the batteries last. They know how to cruise the Internet and can handle electronic gadgetry with skill, but live in a reality where fish are rectangular and eaten with tomato ketchup while whales are animatronic rubbery creatures who are smart enough to sing and play harmonica.

In a few years they will be using mind-changing drugs and be unable to distinguish a multinationally packaged Virtual Reality of cybercops and mutating robo-humanoids from the Real Virtues of Chicken Nuggets and the National Curriculum. Constant vigilance is required if children are not to slip unquestioningly into a world view where nature is an Attenborough video game and networking no more than a computer link-up.

Nor is the search for Realworld just for children. Adult reality is steeped in superstition and prejudice, much of which is constantly reinforced by marketing, advertising, television and the press, However, a great deal of our adult perception of the world simply represents our failure to rethink the things we learned as children.

The ability of mankind to communicate with increasing rapidity around the globe has only increased the speed with which prejudices can fly. Everyone with a message from popes and mullahs to multinational companies can now reach millions of people at once to tell us what we must and must not do to be righteous, to be healthy, to be fashionable or to be green. The means of communication may be post-medieval but many of the messages are neither modern nor enlightened. Christians are still taught that there is Heaven or Hell after death, that sexual activity is sinful except as a reproductive function within marriage and that there is an all-knowing and all-powerful God in charge of everything; oh, yes, and that the dead can be rebooted. ... Other religions peddle similarly outdated and outlandish messages. All these odd beliefs matter because they translate into excuses for persecutory and inhumane activities which are marketed as religious morality for the Righteous In-Crowd and transformed into guilt for the Lapsed and Rebellious.

As a species we may have the technology to reach the moon and to transplant human hearts, but men are still hawking ancient prejudices when they repeat and act on such dangerous nonsense as sexual abuse being more likely to be committed by homosexuals, masturbation making you blind, young girls making better wives if their genitals are mutilated or 'ethnic cleansing' being justifiable.

It is important that as social workers we consciously challenge ourselves to question our learned beliefs. Some of this is easy, and most of us will have recognised by now that our history lessons were underpinned by an anglo centric and imperialist world view, but some of life's messages are subtler and harder to recognise as prejudice. We need to spend time weeding out the unhelpful images we have subconsciously incorporated about disabled children and adults.

Social work is itself an activity whose reality is lost for most people among the convoluted folds of its popular image. Its own divisions and lack of confidence have not done a great deal to help represent it any more accurately. It has been variously described as state interference, a moral activity and an art, all of which contain half truths. Most social workers are state employees, have a code of professional ethics and recognise that human relationships cannot be reduced to scientific style formula. Beyond that, much of what social work does and should be doing is contested and debated both within and outside the work.

There are negative viewpoints at both ends of the political spectrum. The right wing sees social work as an activity which encourages scrounging from the state and discourages people from standing on their own feet. Commentators such as Patrick Minford, Professor of Economics at Liverpool University, include families with disabled children among those who receive too much from the nanny state and who should accept more personal responsibility:

> *'If a family has a handicapped child, for example, they should* ***expect*** *to look after and equip him or her for life as best they could'* (emphasis in the original)
>
> (Minford 1987)

The view from the Left is equally damning. Social work is described as a middle-class profession bathed in mystique which persecutes the working class, removes children from home because of lax housekeeping standards and fails to recognise that many problems arise from societal injustices. Ann Davis, Lecturer in Social Work at Birmingham writes that

> *One of the many* ***hazards*** *that poverty brings is an increased chance of contact with social work* (my emphasis)
>
> (Davis 1987)

These are clearly polarised views, which may have some degree of reality within each of them. It is desirable that we replace them both with a more positive vision.

Neither right nor left see social work as supportive, enabling, helping, representing, acting in partnership, challenging societal expectations or empowering people by encouraging collective action. Yet all these activities have formed part of my experience in working with disabled children and their families, in both the voluntary and statutory sectors. While it is arguable that there may be differences between this marginalised area of work and the mainstream of social work, I am unable to accept that the best practices are not common to all social work. As evidence of this, the following future vision of social work is lifted from Ann Davis. It is written from the perspective of working with adults but it is relatively easy to translate into a child-centred model of social work practice.

> *The future for social work must be in working to encourage the involvement of poor and marginalised groups in society. This can be promoted through social work contact if such contact takes forms which reduce the risk of stigma, pressure to change and marginalisation. The alternatives are to seek to identify and build on people's strengths and talents, increase opportunities for people to meet and work with others who share their oppression and openly share, in negotiations, information about the way in which the state seeks to impose itself on its citizens.*
> (Davis 1987:p 92)

Social work with disabled children should clearly aim to reduce their marginalisation and oppression, and increase their self-esteem. Meeting with other disabled children is clearly important, but to this needs to be added an imperative to include disabled children within the mainstream, not as passive observers but as active participants. An understanding of how the state both defines and disables is a vital step in the struggle for citizenship.

Clients as fellow citizens was very much a 1980s theme just as empowerment and partnership are buzz words for the 1990s. It is easy to caricature these concepts as patronising or unworkable in an unequal society, but they indicate a pattern of social work which is moving in the direction of sharing power and working alongside disadvantaged people. Challenging is also very much a word of the 90's, with everything from vertically to follicly challenged slipping into the tongue-in-cheek vocabulary that so easily becomes standard English.

I see no reason not to join the bandwagon: social workers are personally challenged. Their work involves dealing with their own attitudes and emotions and those of others as well as being very aware of the effect they have on other people. Social work's complexity and difficulty as an activity in a hostile culture are what makes it interesting; its achievements are of value and worth recording and its practitioners deserving of support.

The future is uncertain, and change in the age of the computer is faster than many human beings can keep up with. In an uncertain world, social work needs to hang on to its basic values, but also has to be flexible and willing to change. This means recognising and welcoming new ways of working and forming new alliances in seeking to achieve improvements in people's lives and lifestyles.The profession must be able to reflect on its own practice and learn from that process, but also show an increasing willingness to involve others and to share expertise. Including disabled children in their own struggle is very much a part of this process through listening, counselling, empowering, supporting, sharing knowledge, facilitating contacts with others and protecting from abuse. Social work as a profession must fight for its own right to work in a collaborative manner, toward civil rights, and resist pressures to fragment and become merely the unthinking tool of bureaucracy.

Social work should be seeking to influence legislation and to work creatively within that which exists. The Children Act is open to interpretation, and social workers should maintain pressure to work within it in an opportunistic way which benefits disabled children, seek amendments and suggest improvements when English law is adapted for use in other places such as Scotland or the Isle of Man. Disabled children have rights within the 1986 Disabled Persons Act and within the Education Act 1993, which social work should not allow organisations to bury because of resource issues. Finally, the disability movement continues to push for anti discriminatory legislation based on a social model of disability and which includes disabled children.

Changing the hearts and minds of society and unseating the current establishment may seem long-term, even impossible ambitions, but identifying them as aims gives us a direction in which to work. In the more immediate term, social work can value and share its skills and knowledge, retain its own integrity of purpose and continue to work in the belief that it is possible to help things change for the better.

References and Further Reading.

Baldwin, Sally and Carlisle, Jane (1994) *Social Support for Disabled Children and their Families,* HMSO, London.

Barstow P., Cochrane R and Hur J. (1993) *Evaluation of Conductive Education for children with cerebral palsy*, DFE/University of Birmingham

Beardshaw, Virginia (1993) 'Conductive Education: a rejoinder' in J. Swain, V. Finkelstein, S. French & M. Oliver (eds) *Disabling Barriers – Enabling Environments,* Sage Publications, London.

Begum, Nasa (1994) 'Snow White', in Lois Keith (ed.) *Mustn't Grumble: Writings by Disabled Women,* Women's Press, London.

Beresford, Bryony (1994) *Caring for a Severely Disabled Child,* HMSO, London.

Brown, Christy (1989) *My Left Foot* Penguin Books, Harmondsworth. First edition, Secker and Warburg, London (1954).

Centre for Studies on Inclusive Education (undated leaflet) *Meeting Special Educational Needs,* CSIE

Conan Doyle, Arthur (1975) *The Case Book of Sherlock Holmes* Penguin Books, Harmondsworth. First edition, John Murray (1927)

Darke, Paul Anthony (1994) 'The elephant man [David Lynch, EMI Films, 1980]: an analysis from a disabled perspective', *Disability and Society* 9(3).

Davis, Ann (1987) 'Hazardous lives – social work in the 1980s: a view from the Left' in M. Loney, R. Bocock, J. Clarke, A. Cochrane, P. Graham and M. Wilson, *The State or the Market: Politics and Welfare in Contemporary Britain,* Sage Publications, London.

Department of Health (1991a) *The Children Act 1989 Guidance and Regulations* (9 vols), HMSO, London.

Department of Health (1991b) *The Care of Children: Principles and Practice in Regulations and Guidance,* HMSO, London.

Department of Health (1993) *Children Act Report 1993,* HMSO, London.

Department of Health (1995) *Child Protection: Messages from research,* HMSO, London.

Finch, Janet and Groves, Dulcie (1983) *A Labour of Love: Women, Work and Caring* Routledge & Kegan Paul, London.

Flynn, Margaret (1995) *Personal Communication*

Furneaux, Barbara (1988) *Special Parents* Open University Press

Gazdar, Saleem (1994) 'Young, disabled and black' in *Professional Social Work* October 1994

Glendinning, Caroline (1983) *Unshared Care: parents and their disabled children*, Routledge Kegan Paul, London

Hirst, Michael and Baldwin, Sally (1994) *Unequal Opportunities: Growing up Disabled,* SPRU/HMSO, London.

Home Office/DOH/DES/Welsh Office (1991) *Working Together Under the Children Act 1989: A guide to arrangements for inter agency co operation for the protection of children from abuse,* HMSO, London.

Horwood, William (1987) *Skallagrigg,* Penguin Books, Harmondsworth.

Howitt, Dennis (1995) *Paedophiles and Sexual Offences against Children*, Wiley, Chichester

Keith, Lois (ed.) (1994) *Mustn't Grumble: Writings by disabled women,* Women's Press, London.

Marchant, Ruth and Page, Marcus (1992) *Bridging The Gap,* NSPCC, London.

Middleton, Laura. (1981) *So Much For So Few: A view of sheltered housing* Merseyside Improved Houses. Second revised edition Liverpool University Press, (1987)

Middleton, Laura. (1992) *Children First: Working with children and disability,* Venture Press, Birmingham.

Middleton, Laura (1994) 'Why our childcare services are reinforcing disability,' *Professional Social Work*, October.

Middleton, Laura (1995) 'A disabling childhood', *Childright* Number 113 January/February.

Minford, Patrick (1987) *'The role of the social services: a view from the New Right'* in M. Loney, R. Bocock, J. Clarke, A. Cochrane, P. Graham and M. Wilson, *The State or the Market: Politics and Welfare in Contemporary Britain,* Sage Publications, London.

Morris, Jenny (1991) *Pride against Prejudice: Transforming attitudes to Disability* Women's Press, London.

Morris, Jenny (1993) *Independent Lives: Community Care and Disabled People*, MacMillan, London.

Morris, Jenny (1995) *Gone Missing: Research and Policy Review of disabled children living away from their families* Who Cares Trust, London.

NSPCC (1993) *The ABCD Pack: ABuse and Children Who Are Disabled*, NSPCC, London.

Oliver, Michael (1993) 'Conductive Education: if it wasn't so sad it would be funny' in J. Swain, V. Finkelstein, S, French and M.Oliver (eds.) *Disabling Barriers – Enabling Enviroments*, Sage Publications, London.

Oswin, Maureen (1984) *They Keep Going Away: A critical study of short-term residential care services for children with learning difficulties*, King Edward's Hospital Fund for London.

Parker, Gillian (1993) 'A four-way stretch? the politics of disability and caring',in J. Swain, V. Finkelstein, S. French and M. Oliver (eds.) *Disabling Barriers – Enabling Enviroments*, Sage Publications, London.

Pink, Janice (1994) 'What happened to you?' in Lois Keith (ed.) *Mustn't Grumble: Writings by disabled women,* Women's Press, London.

Rose, Wendy (1995) Assistant Chief Inspector, Social Services Inspectorate, *The Guardian*, 30 May.

Russell, Philippa (1994) *The Children Act 1989; Children and young people with learning disabilities: some opportunities and challenges* National Development Team.

Seedhouse, D (1994) *Fortress NHS,* Wiley, Chichester.

Sefton Social Services (1990) Paper to BASW Annual Conference

Sharland, E., Jones, D., Aldgate, J., Seal, H., and Croucher, M. (1995) *Professional Intervention in Child Sexual Abuse* HMSO, London.

Social Services Inspectorate (1991) *Care Management and Assessment. Practitioner's Guide,* HMSO, London.

Torkington, Ntombenhle Protasia Khotie (1991) *Black Health: A political issue,* Catholic Association for Racial Justice/Liverpool Institute of Higher Education.

Wade, Barrie and Moore, Maggie (1993) *Experiencing Special Education,* Open University Press, Buckingham.

Westcott, Helen. (1993) *Abuse of Children and Adults with Disabilities,* NSPCC, London.

Westcott, Helen. and Cross, Merry. (1995) *This Far and No Further: Towards ending the abuse of disabled children* Venture Press, Birmingham

Woodhouse, Sarah. (1995) 'Child protection and working in partnership with parents', in F. Kaganas, M. King. and C. Piper (eds.) *Legislatng for Harmony:Partnership under the Children Act 1989,* Jessica Kingsley, London and Bristol.